Multilevel Model Foundations

This book introduces the foundations of multilevel models, using Monopoly® rent data, from the classic board game, and the statistical program Stata®. Widespread experience with the game means many readers have a head start on understanding these models. The small dataset, 132 rent values for 22 properties clustered by the four sides of the playing board, combines with extensive graphical displays of data and results so all readers can *see* core multilevel ideas in action at a granular level. Two chapters on standard statistical models, one-way analysis of variance and multiple regression, help readers see how multilevel models rely on but also extend these monolevel ideas. Chapters present three basic multilevel models for cross-sectional analyses – analysis of variance, analysis of covariance, and random coefficients regression – and one basic developmental model for longitudinal analyses. Troubleshooting guidance, combined with close examination of data patterns, and careful inspection of model parameters, all help readers better grasp what model results mean, when model results should or should not be trusted, and how model results link back to core theoretical questions. Consequently, readers will develop a sense of best practices for building and diagnosing their own multilevel models. Those who complete the volume can readily apply what they have learned to more complex datasets and models and adapt available online Stata do files to those projects. Any social scientist working with data clustered in time, in space, or in both, and seeking to learn more about how to use, interpret, or teach these models, will find the book useful.

Ralph B. Taylor is Professor Emeritus of Criminal Justice at Temple University, USA, and a fellow of the American Society of Criminology. He holds a Ph.D. in social psychology from Johns Hopkins University and has authored or co-authored over 90 refereed journal articles in criminal justice, criminology, social psychology, sociology, public health, urban affairs, and law and human behavior. His externally funded research has been supported by the National Science Foundation, the National Institute of Mental Health, the National Institute of Justice, and other sources. He has previously served on the editorial boards of *Criminology and Public Policy, Environment & Behavior, Journal of Criminal Justice, Journal of Quantitative Criminology, Justice Quarterly*, and *Social Psychology Quarterly*. He is the author of *Research Methods in Criminal Justice* (McGraw-Hill, 1994), *Breaking Away from Broken Windows* (Westview, 2001), *Community Criminology* (New York University Press, 2015), and *Human Territorial Functioning* (Cambridge University Press, 1988); the editor of *Urban Neighborhoods* (Praeger, 1986); and a co-editor of *Crime and Justice 2000 Volume 1: Continuities and Change* (National Institute of Justice, 2000). He began teaching multilevel models to graduate students in the late 1990s. Lists of publications and descriptions of research interest areas appear at www.rbtaylor.net.

Multilevel Model Foundations
Monopoly® Data and Stata

Ralph B. Taylor

R Routledge
Taylor & Francis Group

NEW YORK AND LONDON

First published 2024
by Routledge
605 Third Avenue, New York, NY 10158

and by Routledge
4 Park Square, Milton Park, Abingdon, Oxon, OX14 4RN

Routledge is an imprint of the Taylor & Francis Group, an informa business

© 2024 Ralph B. Taylor.

ISBN: 978-1-032-43197-0 (hbk)
ISBN: 978-1-032-49218-6 (pbk)
ISBN: 978-1-003-39268-2 (ebk)

DOI: 10.4324/9781003392682

Typeset in Times New Roman
by Apex CoVantage, LLC

Visit the online material at: www.multilevelmonopolybook.com/

To Michele, of course.
"True riches cannot be bought."
     – Antoine de Saint-Exupéry, *Wind, Sand, and Stars*

Contents

Acknowledgments

Personal and Professional Thanks

The late M. Kay Harris, was a wise, caring, and committed teacher, sane colleague, and friend who insightfully translated compassion into concrete improvements in people's lives more successfully for more decades than anyone I know. She thought this book was a great idea. Thanks for the encouragement Kay.

Stephen Vaisey's summer 2018 Philadelphia workshops pointed attendees to Paul Allison's ideas about fixed effects models. These inform the Chapter 7 discussion of fixed effects versus random effects models.

Many thanks to all the graduate students who, over two decades, both struggled and succeeded in our department's "Stat 2" course. Your queries, frustrations, and enthusiasm about your findings and write-ups all spurred me to work harder toward clearer, more concise, more approachable ways of presenting multilevel models. Students in the 2018 and 2020 offerings of that course worked with earlier iterations of some of the current chapters. They offered positive reactions and helpful suggestions.

At Taylor & Francis, both Elsbeth Wright and Alice Salt proved pivotal in getting the project airborne. Sincere thanks for your advocacy. Ms. Salt and Sophie Ganesh kept it aloft and on course. Their guidance was essential and invaluable.

Professors Steve Abbott and Matthew Richey graciously endorsed the permission granted by the copyright holder of their 1997 article to reproduce landing probabilities from a table in that publication.

Temple University Charles Library professionals Felipe M. Valdez and Olivia Given Castello get a well-deserved thanks and kudos for unearthing crucial Library of Congress resources speedily in response to desperate last minute emails.

Colleague Dr. Jeff Ward taught me tons about Stata over the years and shared his do file template, the front end of which is used, with permission, in the online do files.

Susie Lorand, despite her significant professional, personal, and musical commitments, pried loose time for proofreading the next-to-final version. If it reads cleanly in places, thank her.

The most essential ingredient of all was and still is Michele.

Of course, responsibility for all remaining inaccuracies, unwarranted over-simplifications, and just plain inelegant writing rests solely with the author.

AI statement

The only artificial intelligence (AI) software programs used in the production of this manuscript were the spell checking and grammar checking functions in MS Word 2016.

Crediting Sources or Third Party Material

MONOPOLY® & © 2022 Hasbro, Inc. Used with permission.

Table 10.1 is sourced from Table 3, Abbott, S. D., & Richey, M. (1997). Take a walk on the Boardwalk. *The College Mathematics Journal*, *28*(3), 162–171. https://doi.org/10.2307/2687519, copyright © 1997 Mathematical Association of America, reprinted by permission of Taylor & Francis Ltd, www.tandfonline.com on behalf of Mathematical Association of America, and of the authors.

Acronyms and Abbreviations

ANCOVA analysis of covariance
ANOVA analysis of variance
HLM hierarchical linear model(s)
RCR random coefficient regression
SES socioeconomic status

Password for Online Data File

TheRevolutionWillNotBeTelevised
www.multilevelmonopolybook.com/

1 First Steps

First Things

First things first. This book is not just about "stats." It is about statistics and theory. More specifically, how to carefully test a theory and elaborate it in a multilevel context. This is not just about "stats."

Instructors

Instructors in social sciences considering assigning this volume might wonder: why this introduction to multilevel models rather than another?

(1) It uses a dataset, from the board game Monopoly®, with which many readers are already familiar. Their prior acquaintance makes learning key ideas easier. They can observe novel operations, like empirical Bayes estimation or random coefficients regression, applied at a granular level to known entities.

(2) On occasion, one finds misunderstood multilevel modeling operations in published research articles in high quality refereed journals. Readers are warned about such missteps. Two examples: random intercept models fail to control for between-group differences, and group mean centering does not remove between-group compositional differences.

(3) Despite the straightforward structure of the dataset – 132 rent values spread across 22 properties on four sides of the playing board – it proves pedagogically useful for readers in two ways, beyond its baseline familiarity for many. It reveals oddities, like negative level-2 R^2 values. Although these can occur with multilevel models, they are not covered in most introductory texts. Furthermore, the dataset harbors flaws. Although experienced instructors can foresee them, the faults remain concealed from most student modelers until they launch diagnostic protocols. The broader pedagogical lesson is this. Sometimes, even though standard model selection decision-making aids and results point to a preferred model, looking "under the hood" of various models may

DOI: 10.4324/9781003392682-1

unearth concerns. Two chapters containing models with highly collinear estimated parameters present cases in point. Readers are encouraged to trust the model investigation process before trusting model results.

(4) Readers can readily adapt snippets of code in the online supporting Stata do files to analyze their own datasets.

(5) The volume ramps up slowly, moving systematically from monolevel ANOVA and multiple regression models to multilevel models.

(6) The emphasis on the constant dialectic between model parameters, theory constructs, and theory dynamics, encourages readers to be ever mindful of why specific parameters merit model inclusion, and how different model parameters relate to one another.

(7) The volume includes one chapter for multilevel models of longitudinal data.

Students and Other Interested Readers

For students and other interested readers: (1) Read this book to learn the basic ideas behind multilevel models. These analytics have many names: hierarchical linear models or HLM, mixed effects models, random effects models, and random coefficients regression or RCR models. They are all in the same family. (2) Read to learn how these models can help test and elaborate theories of interest and evaluate programs and policies. (3) Read to learn how to do. As American philosopher John Dewey said long ago, we learn best by doing. Run the Stata programs, available online at multilevelmonopolybook.com, examine results, and adapt code snippets to run programs on your own datasets.

Key Volume Features

There are three.

(1) Throughout, only one simple dataset, and one outcome variable, appears in all examples. The set contains rent due values for properties from the US 65th Edition Parker Brothers Monopoly® board game. Figure 1.1 shows a picture of the deed for Boardwalk. Rent charged to the player landing on the space ranges from $50 to $2,000 in 1935 dollars, depending on its level of real estate development. Rent is the outcome of interest throughout. Readers already familiar with the basic elements of the dataset – properties, how they differ around the board, rents, hotels, and guesthouses – can speedily grasp underlying statistical ideas.

The main data file available online also includes 2022 inflation-adjusted rent values. A $2,000 rental payment in 1935 is equivalent, after adjusting for inflation, to a payment of $43,165.52 in November 2022. Use the 2022 rent values as an alternate outcome, rerun the programs for each chapter with that outcome, and practice interpreting output. Advantages and disadvantages, clarified in the next section, follow from this diminutive dataset.

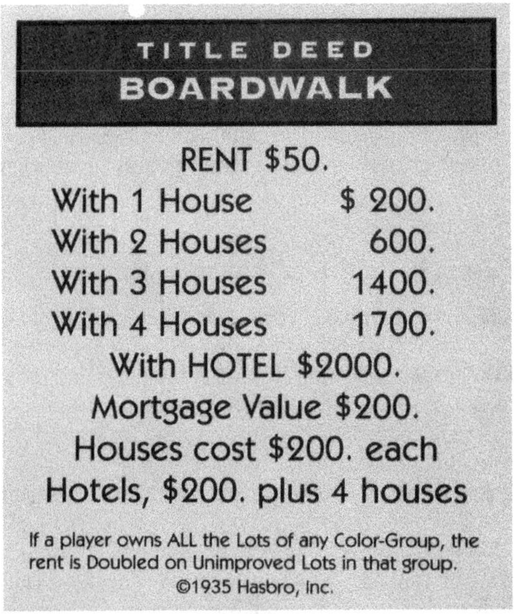

Figure 1.1 Boardwalk deed.

Source: Photo by author. MONOPOLY® and © 2022 Hasbro, Inc. Used with permission.

(2) The approach uses the statistical program Stata.

(3) The volume focuses only on the fundamental features of multilevel models.

Toy Datasets

The benefits of learning technical topics using a toy dataset can be seen in the online appendix detailing how the Monopoly® game and its data have been used in college classrooms to illustrate important social problems, like gender inequality. In short, Monopoly already has been put to use teaching serious topics in higher education.

The toy dataset does have limitations, such as a limited number of neighborhoods. Such data constraints, however, enable readers to more speedily grasp multilevel model fundamentals, and observe how, even with simple data and relatively simple questions, modeling results can mislead. Understanding the basic multilevel models with such a simple dataset readies readers for engaging with datasets that are more complex and deploying more elaborate multilevel models.

Does working with a toy dataset now make it more challenging, later, to apply lessons learned to more complex datasets later? Perhaps, and those challenges are directly addressed here. The volume and online do files both provide tips and illustrate needed systematic approaches. For example, extensive graphical displays of both data and results facilitate the get acquainted process and help modelers more speedily "see" what the models are doing.

Using and Going Beyond This Volume

How to most productively use, and then go beyond, multilevel modeling with the Monopoly dataset? Run the online program for each chapter as you read. Generate all the results appearing here. Run the programs for the inflation-adjusted outcome, rent2022, and interpret results. Take snippets of Stata program files, and adapt them to your own dataset for your own project. Run code, get results, and then interpret.

One last orienting word: you may be able to skip ahead. Other introductory books on multilevel models (Bickel, 2006; Finch et al., 2019; Garson, 2019; Luke, 2004; Robson & Pevalin, 2016) transition quickly from basic regression or analysis of variance models to multilevel models. This volume, in contrast, spends considerable time on those transitions. Ignore early chapters if you already have a solid understanding of regression and one-way analysis of variance.

Troubleshooting Mixed-Model Mayhem

To get the most out of the volume and avoid mishaps: build slowly, look carefully at results, and deliberately cross-reference model results to observable data patterns. Chapters with more complex multilevel models include step-by-step troubleshooting guides. Whether working with a Monopoly® dataset, the US Census, a multistage-clustered sample survey, or the Pathways to Desistance dataset (Fine et al., 2021), the basic ideas are the same, and the ways you can go wrong are the same. The lessons reviewed here apply broadly.

The Cost in Coverage

The focus on foundations, of course, comes at a cost. This is not a comprehensive book on multilevel modeling. For example, there is no discussion here of models for different types of outcomes, like count variables; more complex models, like those with mediating dynamics; or models with measurement as one level of a model. The last chapter suggests numerous excellent sources for exploring topics that are more advanced.

What Are Multilevel Data?

Multilevel data are comprised of records that (a) are clustered and (b) capture observations spanning either different spatial, or temporal, or spatiotemporal units (Baumer & Arnio, 2012). "Clustered" means that individual observations belong to larger groups of observations, each group sharing some common attribute. For a cross-sectional spatial example, residents in a city surveyed about local police practices may include subsets of surveyed residents living in the same police district, thus sharing the same local living conditions, and dealing with the same district-level policing organization (Taylor et al., 2010). In this example, surveyed residents represent the level-1 units and police districts represent level-2 units. Level-1 units are clustered within level-2 units.

For a longitudinal example, adolescents may be surveyed repeatedly over several years on their views about the legitimacy of law (Kaiser & Reisig, 2017). Different observations over time from the same person have something in common. Therefore, responses over time are clustered by individuals. Observations from each individual at each point in time are the level-1 units, and the respondents themselves are the level-2 units. Multilevel models allow charting "pathways through time" (Raudenbush, 2005) for each individual's responses.

Both these examples represent perfect hierarchies: each level-1 unit belongs to one and only one level-2 unit. Multilevel models also can tackle "imperfect hierarchies" (Snijders & Bosker, 2012, p. 205).[1]

Monopoly rent values for a single property, like those shown on the Boardwalk property deed in the previous section, could be clustered spatially in a number of ways: by property name ($n = 22$ groups of six rents each), by color code ($n = 8$ groups of 12 or 18 rents each), or by side of the playing board ($n = 4$ groups of 30 or 36 rents each). The multilevel cross-sectional chapters adopt the latter grouping of level-1 rent values into four level-2 groups, treating each side of the playing board as a different neighborhood.

In datasets with sufficient numbers of level-1 cases, and sufficient numbers of groups at level 2 or level 3, clustering can happen at more than one level. For example, survey respondents (level 1) could be clustered within different neighborhoods (level 2), and neighborhoods could be clustered within different cities (level 3). Sometimes, level 1 can be a measurement level (Sampson et al., 1997).

Here, in the spatial analyses, level-1 units correspond to specific rent values on property deeds. The six values represent six stages of real estate development on, for example, six different streetblocks, where a streetblock is the two sides of a street between cross streets, along that named street. The 132 level-1 rent values are clustered in turn into four level-2 units, one for each of the four different sides of the board. Each side of the board corresponds *roughly* to different neighborhoods or districts within Atlantic City.[2] Temporal analyses cluster the rent values in a different manner.

Why Are Multilevel Analyses Needed for Multilevel Data?

If working with clustered or multilevel data, does one *really* need these models? Why not just tweak conventional, monolevel statistical models?

Consider two sets of issues. The first is technical. (1) Clustered data properties may not align with monolevel model assumptions. Further, (2) mixed models adjust each data cluster in light of dataset-wide cluster properties. This might be important.

The second set of issues is theoretical. Multilevel models open up new possibilities. (3) Initially, they separate outcome variation into multiple buckets, one for each level. This helps clarify the scales at which specific dynamics might be operating. (4) A level-1 predictor's impact on an outcome may depend on level-2 context. In many social science disciplines, including criminology (Wilcox et al., 2003), public health (Diez Roux & Mair, 2010), demography (Entwisle, 2007), and social psychology (Pettigrew, 2018), to name just a few, multilevel models open up new lines of inquiry which may prove theoretically consequential. Although cross-level interaction impacts can be investigated in monolevel models, multilevel models provide some advantages.

How Much Stata Should You Know Before Starting This Book?

A successful learning experience is more likely for those with at least one course in Stata in which they learned basic features of the interface, data files, do or program files, and log or output files. Those without such a course, however, can quickly get up to speed by systematically working through an introductory book on Stata like Acock (2018), Longest (2014), or Kohler and Kreuter (2012).

Another way to get up to speed is to work systematically through the Stata channel videos on youtube.com. Those videos with "interface" "data management" and "Tour of" in their titles may prove especially helpful.

You need access to the Stata program to open up the main dataset and run the programs in each chapter. For students in the US, as of this writing, a basic six-month Stata license is $48 (www.stata.com/order/new/edu/profplus/student-pricing/).

How Much Statistics Should You Know Before Starting This Book?

The following are essential:

- familiarity with basic descriptive statistics: measures of central tendency (mean, mode, median), dispersion (standard deviation, variance, standard

errors, confidence intervals, maybe sum of squared differences), and association (correlation, maybe covariation);
- at least some exposure to statistical inference and ideas about hypothesis testing; and
- familiarity with, or willingness to get quickly up to speed on, graphical data displays, including histograms, box-and-whisker plots, clustered bar charts, and scatterplots.

The following are strongly recommended:

- acquaintanceship with the basics of bivariate and multivariate linear (ordinary least squares or OLS) regression, including

  - *b* weights,
  - beta weights,
  - constants,
  - scatterplots of regression lines, and
  - R squared (R^2) values.

- exposure to related statistics including

  - *t* tests and analysis of variance (ANOVA).

Experience with the following would be nice:

- F test of R^2
- standard errors of *b* weights,
- *t* tests of *b* or beta weights,
- residuals,
- predicted scores,
- residual diagnostics, and
- tests for linear vs. curvilinear impacts.

If not sure about readiness, just try it. Since the focus is on fundamentals, some basic things like sums of squared differences will be covered. The basic points covered may be new for some and review for others. Either way, dive right in. If the going gets too tough, put it on pause, go to other sources, and fill in gaps. If it is too easy, zoom ahead.

How Does This Book Differ From Other Basic Introductions to Multilevel Models?

Other introductions to multilevel modeling include Luke (2004), Bickel (2006), Finch et al. (2019), Garson (2019), and Robson and Pevalin (2016). This volume differs in important ways from each.

First, this volume spends more time explaining some fundamentals. The goal is to construct a sturdy bridge from basic statistical models like OLS multiple regression and one-way ANOVA, to related ideas in multilevel modeling.

Second, as already explained, this volume relies on a familiar dataset with only 132 records.

Third, readers can see how specific model parameters link to specific data points or groups of data points.

Fourth, the current approach is one of progressive elaboration. New ideas and new models are rolled out slowly.

Fifth, this volume illustrates how multilevel models apply to longitudinal data. Some introductory volumes do not. Multilevel models are proving an important tool for investigating longitudinal data (Twisk, 2013). This volume displays some of those possibilities.

Sixth, as mentioned previously for instructors, this volume carefully explains several points not well covered in other introductory volumes, such as negative level-2 R^2, sometimes hard-to-detect problems created by collinear parameter estimates, what is controlled for in a random intercepts model versus a fixed effects model with dummy variables for level-2 groups, and more.

Who Should Read This Book?

The intended audience includes, in the social sciences, advanced undergraduates, graduate students at any level, and postdoctoral researchers who are working with clustered or longitudinal data.

It also includes social science evaluation researchers and policy analysts, as well as program directors, who need to make sense of clustered or longitudinal quantitative data from a social program, and evaluators assessing program delivery to different places or organizations.

For all these intended audiences, time with this book might facilitate understanding others' analyses and/or enhance their own.

Online Appendices

Online appendices are found at multilevelmonopolybook.com.

Two files are just for those seeking additional scholarly background. One recounts a trans-Atlantic scholarly tiff in the first half of the 20th century. At issue: potential confusion between results from level-1 units and results from level-2 units. The second sketches scholarship examining the contested origins of Monopoly and notes scholarship on the uses of Monopoly in college classrooms.

A ZIP file contains the main data file, programs for different chapters, and log output files. A password is needed to open the data file. The password – The

`RevolutionWillNotBeTelevised` – also appears at the front of the volume.

Run the programs (`*.do`) to reproduce the results seen in each chapter and some unseen ones as well. Check results against the provided output (`*.log`) files. Open both `do` and `log` files with a plain text editor like Notepad++. For best learning, run the program at the beginning of a chapter and review your own output as you read along. Then, run each program again but use the inflation-adjusted rent variable, `rent2022`, instead. Interpret your new output.

Upcoming Chapters

Chapter 2 introduces the Monopoly® dataset, explains how the rent values shown on the property deeds have been organized, and considers different identifying variables constructed from card information.

Chapter 3 gathers basic descriptive information about the dataset, deploying Stata commands including `summarize`, `describe`, and `codebook`.

Many others, and I, recommend conducting "plain" single-level or monolevel multiple regressions before launching multilevel models. Chapter 4 takes that idea to heart, running ordinary least squares (OLS) simple regressions predicting rent with different status variables. Predicted scores and residuals are generated, along with a table of statistical results.

Chapter 5 deploys models with which you already are familiar, ANOVA and monolevel regression, to estimate rent impacts of socioeconomic status (SES) captured by position on one of the four sides of the game board. These models *start* to bring into focus a key multilevel modeling question: Where is the outcome variation? How much is within groups? How much is between groups?

Chapter 6 describes the most basic multilevel model. It is so basic *it does not even have any predictors*. Two simple, readily grasped equations explain what the model is doing. A simple graphical data display shows how multilevel models "learn" from all the data in the dataset, in turn adjusting outcome scores in each specific group. This technique is called empirical Bayes estimation.

Chapter 7 explains multilevel models with level-1 fixed effects, that is, the model includes only level-1 predictors, and each predictor is allowed to have only one average impact on rent. The questions motivating this model are explained by referencing analysis of covariance (ANCOVA) ideas. These suggest two different types of questions for investigation. Different ways to think about R^2 with multilevel models are contemplated.

Chapter 8 introduces random coefficient regression models. These generate a useful model for deciding whether to launch an empirical investigation into theorized cross-level interaction effects in a cross-sectional context. A cross-level interaction in this context usually means the impact of a level-1 variable on an outcome depends on scores for a level-2 variable. The level-2 attribute shapes whether the level-1 variable has a stronger or weaker impact on the outcome. Saying that a hotel's rent impact depends on the SES of the neighborhood is an example. This chapter charts the investigative steps, empirically documenting the initial stages of the inquiry. Detailed model checks reveal an unwelcome surprise and require revisiting model choices.

Chapter 9 switches from space to space-time. Longitudinal multilevel models clarify temporal trends in development-driven rent escalation, and how these might vary depending on location. This is another instance of theorizing and testing a cross-level interaction. Saying that each property charted its own pathway of real estate development through time, and the latter depended on neighborhood SES, is an example. The dataset gains a hypothetical year variable reflecting the points in time each property deed attained a particular level of real estate development. Again, detailed model checks cause consternation about the chosen model, and require reconsidering what is the optimal model.

Chapter 10 introduces different transformations applicable to level-1 predictors: grand mean centering, group mean centering, and multileveling. What does each involve? How is each done? More importantly, considering both theory and analyses, why is each done? Theoretical matters loom large for the latter two transforms. Current debate about centering, and a common misunderstanding of what group mean centering does and does not do, are both briefly noted.

Chapter 11 suggests next steps. Recommended readings and next steps are noted. Even though it is a big step to go from mining the "toy" dataset deployed here to tackling "real" datasets, and a multilevel model with many more moving parts might be the future focus, the type of modeling sequences and investigative protocols described here still apply. Trust the process.

Now, it is time to meet the dataset and consider property deed names in the context of early 20th century Atlantic City, New Jersey.

Notes

1 The cross-classified model, the multiple membership model, and the multiple membership multiple classification models each represent examples of such imperfect hierarchies. With a cross-classified model, an observation, such as a person, belongs to two different types of units, and both types are at the same level. For example, you may have juveniles adjudicated delinquent who live in different neighborhoods and attend different programs (Lockwood, 2012). This would be a cross-classified model. Browne and colleagues (2001) address multiple membership multiple classification (MMMC) models.
2 Marvin Gardens is an exception since it is in the neighboring town of Margate, New Jersey.

2 From Title Deeds to Dataset

Take a Look

Look at Figure 2.1. The aero view reflects what Atlantic City, New Jersey, looked like from the air in 1910. The arrow placed on the map points to Mediterranean Avenue. Notice there is not much development along Mediterranean Avenue. Then find the Boardwalk, the wide strip between the dark seawall marking the shore side end of the beach, and the big hotels facing that strip. Note Boardwalk's proximity not only to the beach and cooling afternoon onshore breezes off the Atlantic Ocean, but also to the entertainment piers at bottom center and bottom right stretching out into that ocean.

A close examination of the corresponding digital image file reveals *every developable property on the Monopoly playing board* save Marvin Gardens.[1] The game deeds reference locatable geographic features that existed in real neighborhoods.

Now, a thought experiment. "August, the last month of the summer in Atlantic City, is also a moderately hot month, with an average temperature fluctuating between 72°F (22.2°C) and 79.7°F (26.5°C)."[2] If staying there for a short summer vacation in August, in the pre-air conditioning, pre-television, pre-digital distraction decades of the early 20th century, where would you rather stay? On the Boardwalk with cooling afternoon breezes and numerous nearby entertainment venues? Or on Mediterranean Avenue, many blocks back from the beach, and the afternoon onshore breezes? If you would rather stay along the Boardwalk, how much more would you be willing to pay?

In short, names of cheap versus expensive properties on the playing board correspond with cheap versus expensive places to stay in 1920s Atlantic City. Price differences were driven by geographic differences. More broadly, these geographic differences created differences in the desirability or socioeconomic status (SES) of various Atlantic City neighborhoods. The game's creators encoded those SES differences into three game features: (1) relative position along the playing board, (2) prices to develop real estate, and ultimately, (3) rent prices.

DOI: 10.4324/9781003392682-2

Figure 2.1 Location of Mediterranean Avenue (arrow) in 1910 Atlantic City.

Source: Library of Congress. Map: Aero view of Atlantic City, 1910. Retrieved January 5, 2023, from www.loc.gov/resource/g3814a.pm005090/; digital id: http://hdl.loc.gov/loc.gmd/g3814a. pm005090/

Rents

Figure 2.2 shows the first six rows in the Monopoly dataset, for Mediterranean Avenue. The right-most column, rent, captures the six rent prices ranging from $2 to $250, shown on the property deed card.[3]

Houses and Hotels

Note the two variables just to the left of the rent values: n_house and hotel. These reflect the stage of real estate property development on the property. The latter is a dummy variable with values of only 0 or 1. In the first five records, there is no hotel, so hotel = 0. In the sixth record, the hotel has been built and hotel = 1. As Monopoly players know, all properties of the same color must be owned by one player before any real estate development can begin, and all properties of the same color must have four guesthouses before a hotel can be built on any one of the properties in the color group.

	ave_name	ave_colr	side	sequence	seq_zero	ave_colr1	ave_colr0	sidezero	purchase	n_house	hotel	rent
1	Mediterranean	purple	1	1	0	1	0	0	60	0	0	2
2	Mediterranean	purple	1	1	0	1	0	0	60	1	0	10
3	Mediterranean	purple	1	1	0	1	0	0	60	2	0	30
4	Mediterranean	purple	1	1	0	1	0	0	60	3	0	90
5	Mediterranean	purple	1	1	0	1	0	0	60	4	0	160
6	Mediterranean	purple	1	1	0	1	0	0	60	0	1	250

Figure 2.2 How property deed data are organized in dataset: entries for Mediterranean Avenue.

To the left of the hotel variable is a count variable for the number of guesthouses; it ranges from 0 to 4. Rent goes up with each additional house.[4]

Moreover, as Monopoly players well know, the rent jump from four guesthouses to a hotel is the steepest; here it is $90. The n_house variable reverts to 0 when a hotel is present, because the player must tear down all guesthouses to make room for a hotel. It is also 0 when the property is unimproved and visitors are just camping out.

Finally, again as experienced players know, it costs more to purchase properties, and to finance development, for building guesthouses and hotels, in higher priced neighborhoods further along the playing board.

Identifying Information

At the leftmost side of the records, two variables identify the particular property. The variable ave_name provides the name of the street in question. The variable ave_colr describes the color for that group of properties. Baltic and Mediterranean Avenues are in the purple group of properties.

Position or Socioeconomic Status (SES) Variables

Several variables in the dataset reflect the relative SES position of the individual property on the playing board. SES is lowest right after the "GO" or starting location, and highest just before it. All of these ordinal variables are simply different reflections of the SES of the particular property. The variables offer anywhere from 4 to 22 ordered classifications for SES.

At the most granular level, the variable sequence references the order in which the property is encountered as one moves clockwise around the board, starting from "GO." One is Mediterranean Avenue; 22 is the Boardwalk.

Another version of the sequence variable is seq_zero. It is exactly the same variable except that it starts with 0 (Mediterranean Avenue), going up only to 21 (Boardwalk). Having a version of this and the other SES variables starting at 0 rather than 1 will provide certain interpretive advantages, described later.

Two variables reference the color scheme ordering: ave_colr1 and ave_colr0 as one moves around the playing board. The first variable, `ave_colr1`, is equal to 1 for the two purple properties, Baltic Avenue and Mediterranean Avenue. It is equal to 8 for the royal blue properties, Park Place and Boardwalk. The variable `ave_colr0` is the same as `ave_colr1` but starts at 0 rather than 1 and only goes up to 7.

Two numeric variables reflect the side of the playing board on which the property is located: `side` and `sidezero`. The variable `side` starts at 1, flips to 2 after passing "In Jail," flips to 3 after passing "Free Parking," and flips to 4 after passing "Go to Jail"; `sidezero` starts at 0 and ends at 3.

Each location-linked indicator is ordinal. Higher numbers indicate a location further along the board and, therefore, higher development costs and higher rents charged. The rent increase when jumping one status level, for any of these variables, can vary depending on where one is in the ordering before jumping.

The Same Variables Are Also Neighborhood SES Identifiers

In short, these three variables, reflecting game board geography, group named properties into neighborhoods of varying SES in historical Atlantic City (Choldin, 2019/1984; Choldin et al., 1980; Gans, 1967; Mckenzie, 1923; Warner, 1962).[5] Each variable roughly reflects that property's relative community socioeconomic standing. In urban and suburban contexts, spatial communities exist at multiple, nested layers. Layers range in size from the streetblock up to a section of the city (Suttles, 1972). Here too one can choose different layers of community from the named property up to the side of the playing board.

The following details further support this correspondence between neighborhood SES differences in early 20th century Atlantic City geography, and the property-ordering, SES-reflecting variables on the playing board. (1) Avenues next to each other and in the same color group on the board were sometimes geographically proximate in early 20th century Atlantic City. Examples include Mediterranean and Baltic; Park Place and Boardwalk; Indiana, Illinois, and Kentucky; and New York, St. James Place, and Kentucky. (2) All named properties on the fourth side of the playing board – Boardwalk, Park Place, (South) North Carolina Avenue, Pacific Avenue, and (South) Pennsylvania Avenue have streetblocks no more than a few hundred feet from the beach and the ocean. (3) Historically, all of the named properties on the first side of the board were either well away from the ocean-fronting beach (Mediterranean, Baltic), or in the relatively less-developed-at-the-time northeast section of the ocean beachfront (Oriental, Vermont), or proximate to less disadvantaged neighborhoods in the northern section of the city (Connecticut) (Johnson, 2009, p. 50).

Time to examine the entire dataset descriptively and statistically in Chapter 3.

Notes

1 Marvin Gardens was and is a neighborhood in Margate, New Jersey.
2 www.weather-us.com/en/new-jersey-usa/atlantic-city-weather-august.
3 Despite diligent searching, I have been unable to learn if the rents shown are for a week or a month.
4 Although for simplification of pedagogy the rent impact of each additional guesthouse is treated as a linear relationship, it is nonlinear. Rent increases with additional guesthouses are steeper the more guesthouses already present.
5 Bearing in mind the Margate, New Jersey, exception for Marvin Gardens.

3 Describing the Dataset Statistically

In many social science disciplines, empirical quantitative journal articles include a table of descriptive statistics for the variables used. This chapter describes generating such a table using variables from the Monopoly data and Stata commands.

This and other chapters show results from running Stata programs, called do files.[1] The dataset and the programs are available online in a password protected zip file at multilevelmonopolybook.com. Each chapter with analyses has its own do file.

Getting to Know New Data

With a new data file, assume nothing. Investigate everything. This rule applies whether the dataset is one that you and colleagues generate, or one downloaded from an external site. Closely scrutinize all available documentation, including codebooks. Next, for each variable that will appear in analyses, *drill down* and carefully inspect *everything*.

Start with descriptive statistics. For each variable: examine patterns of missing data; know what different missing data values mean; and inspect all descriptive statistics including – as appropriate depending on the level of measurement – minimum and maximum values, standard deviations, means and medians, skewness statistics, and useful percentile values (5th, 10th, 25th, 75th, 90th, 95th). Give all value labels a close read.

Then, inspect variable distributions visually. Plot each variable appearing in analyses using histograms; box-and-whisker plots, a.k.a. boxplots; or stem-and-leaf plots. These plots provide a tremendous amount of information in a compact format (Chambers et al., 1983; Tukey, 1977). Boxplots prove particularly useful. "Sometimes unexpected features such as outliers, skew or differences in spread are made obvious by boxplots but might otherwise go unnoticed" (Hamilton, 1992, p. 10). The boxplot for rent, for example, reveals one outlier value and suggests a somewhat positively skewed distribution.

DOI: 10.4324/9781003392682-3

Take your time. *Look closely.* Become an expert on distributions of scores for each specific variable to be included in analyses. If models deployed assume a normally distributed outcome variable, check skewness and kurtosis statistics as well as graphical displays of the variable. Is this assumption met?

Stata provides three commands for learning about all the variables in the dataset:

- `summarize`
- `describe`
- `codebook`

Use all of them and carefully examine results. The first provides basic statistics. The second provides variable names and variable labels. The third describes missing data patterns as well as value labels for specific scores on specific variables.

Open up the data file itself and *look* at the data to understand how they are organized. Click on the data view icon at the top of your Stata (version 18) main page to look at the data file once it is open. The icon is a table of data with a magnifying glass hovering over it. Once opened, data should look exactly like the data layout in Figure 2.2.

Getting Data Patterns Down in Black and White

An initial table of descriptive statistics for predictor and outcome variables serves three important purposes in a journal article. (1) It allows readers to get closer to and better understand the data. (2) Other researchers may seek to replicate published work. Once they have the data file and the corresponding variables, they can check their descriptive statistics against those published in the original report. Cross-referencing initial descriptive statistics with those an independent researcher obtains provides an important quality check for any later work. (3) Reviewers examining an article submitted for potential publication in a scholarly journal may harbor suspicions about the submission's data. Checking descriptive statistics may help allay concerns. Alternatively, it may deepen them. Journal reviewers with experience in a particular field of scholarship can look at descriptive statistics in a submitted manuscript and quickly spot problems. With problems come doubts. In short, there is a lot at stake here. Get it right.

Consequently, it is *crucial* to *never rekey* when generating a table of descriptive statistics. Automate the process to make it as clean as possible. The online `do` file generates a table of descriptive statistics you can put into Word or Excel in order to format a table, like Table 3.1.

Variables appear in three groups: the outcome variable, `rent`, in 1935 and inflation-adjusted November 2022 values; features linked to the street's location on the board; and features reflecting levels of development.

Table 3.1 Descriptive statistics: Variables in Monopoly® dataset

Variable	Variable name	n	min	max	mean	SD	p50	skew
Outcome variables								
Rent due, 1935	rent	132	$2	$2,000	$469.1	$451.7	$325.0	0.86
Rent inflation adjusted to 2022	rent2022	132	$43.1	$43,146.5	$10,119.2	$9,745.2	$7,011.3	0.86
Predictor variables: Fixed at property level								
Property sequence: start at 1	sequence	132	1	22	11.5	6.4	11.5	0
Property sequence: start at 0	seq_zero	132	0	21	10.5	6.4	10.5	0
Property color: start at 1	ave_colr1	132	1	8	4.5	2.2	4.5	0
Property color: start at 0	ave_colr0	132	0	7	3.5	2.2	3.5	0
Side of board: start at 1	side	132	1	4	2.5	1.1	2.5	0
Side of board: start at 0	sidezero	132	0	3	1.5	1.1	1.5	0
Purchase price	purchase	132	$60	$400	$208.6	$92.4	$210	0.2
Predictor variables: Level of development								
N of houses present	n_house	132	0	4	1.7	1.5	1.5	0.3
Hotel present (1)/ not (0)	hotel	132	0	1	0.2	0.4	0	1.8

Source: Monopoly® game board and game cards. *Note*: Each property deed appears six times in the dataset: once with a hotel, and five times with no hotel. When no hotel is present, there may be anywhere from zero to four guesthouses on the property. For the sequence, color, and side of board variables, higher score indicates further from the game starting square ("GO").

Note

1 Long (2009) provides excellent suggestions about broader matters such as organizing computer workspace, directory structures, file naming, and more. Those matters are not covered here.

4 Monolevel Models Part I

OLS (Ordinary Least Squares) Regression

Run Monolevel Models Before Multilevel Models

The question considered here is this. Using ordinary least squares (OLS) monolevel regression, how does SES, linked to either a specific property deed or its neighborhood, affect rent? The monolevel, simple regression models shown here ignore several data features: multiple rent values linked to a single title deed; different title deeds sharing the same color scheme; and multiple title deeds located on the same side of the board, that is, in the same neighborhood. Nonetheless, the model generates initial answers to this question. Regardless of the type of outcome variable, conduct initial monolevel models *before* running multilevel ones.

Why? Simply this: monolevel results provide a comparative baseline. This first look at predictor–outcome links sets a ballpark expectation about what later multilevel models might show. It is easy to make mistakes when setting up multilevel models. Monolevel results from properly specified models can be compared against corresponding multilevel results. Although results from the two types of models of course will differ in important ways, if a comparison reveals wildly divergent findings that may be a clue to an improperly specified multilevel model.

The Question

Three variables serve as proxies for the relative community SES linked with the named Monopoly® property: its position in the sequence of all properties, its position in the color series, and the side of the playing board where it is located. For each, higher numbers reflect a later position in the sequence and higher SES. Which operationalization of SES better predicts rent?

One Preliminary Matter: Do Tests of Statistical Significance "Make Sense" When Using Population Data?

This Monopoly dataset provides a full *population* of rent values. It includes all named properties on the board, under all stages of real estate development.

DOI: 10.4324/9781003392682-4

Statistical inference, however, is about making inferences from samples back to populations from which samples were drawn (Blalock, 1979, p. 5). If the population rather than a sample is being analyzed, should we be examining statistical significance like *t* tests and *F* tests *at all*?

Researchers routinely ignore this concern and apply tests of statistical significance to population data. Social scientists have differed on the wisdom of this since at least the 1960s (Blalock, 1979, pp. 241–243). The disagreement continues today in discussions of *p*-hacking and the replication crisis in social psychology (Gelman, 2018) and in controversies about publishing significance tests (Trafimow & Marks, 2015). Those important matters aside, the basic question here is this: in what way, with population data like these Monopoly data, does statistical significance make sense?

Consider Blalock's stance on this question "There is a way of looking at tests of significance [with population data] that is much more compatible with theoretical explanations as to *why* a particular relationship has been found" (Blalock, 1979, p. 242). If researchers are interested in causal dynamics, rather than mere "generalizations to fixed populations," a statistically significant impact of a predictor on an outcome using population data allows the researcher to rule out "the simple 'chance-processes' alternative" (Blalock, 1979, p. 242). Could the observed connections have arisen from data composed of independent random variables, linked to one another only by random processes? Finding statistical significance suggests not.

Statistical significance, of course, "will *not* rule out many other kinds of alternative explanations" (Blalock, 1979, p. 243). It only allows ruling out the idea that the connections observed arose *just* from "chance-processes." In other words, if the impact of *X* on *Y* is statistically significant with population data, there are underlying processes creating that link. Such a connection is likely *not* driven *solely* by randomness, or noise, in the data.

Another Preliminary Matter: Does the Outcome Distribution Match Model Assumptions?

Following Chapter 3's advice about looking carefully reveals a skewness statistic for `rent` of 0.86. This value suggests the distribution is "moderately skew," that is, somewhat non-symmetrical and slightly non-normal (Bulmer, 1967, p. 63). "A distribution with a skewness greater than 1 in absolute value [is seen] as highly skew" (Bulmer, 1967, p. 63). In short, the form of the outcome departs somewhat from model assumptions. Whether to do something about this, and if so what, is taken up in Chapter 8.

Running SES Regressions

Table 4.1 displays results from three different regressions, one for each version of the SES variable, using the code in the online `do` file.[1] The code uses

Table 4.1 Monolevel regressions predicting rent with SES predictors

		Model 1 (seq_zero)	Model 2 (ave_colr0)	Model 3 (sidezero)
Predictor				
Relative prop-	b	$31.917		
erty position	(se)	($5.556)		
	t	5.745		
	p	< .001		
Avenue color	b		$93.972	
sequence	(se)		($16.423)	
	t		5.722	
	p		< .001	
Side of board	b			$180.719
	(se)			($33.056)
	t			5.467
	p			< .001
Intercept		$133.936	$140.158	$197.982
N observations		132	132	132
R-squared		0.202	0.201	0.187
F statistic		33.003	32.741	29.888

Note: Three ordinary least squares (OLS) bivariate regression models. Model 1 uses the sequence variable starting at 0 (0–21). Model 2 uses the color sequence variable starting at 0 (0–7). Model 3 uses the side of the board variable, starting at 0 (0–3).

the SES variables with valid zero values, making the constant/intercept interpretable. Some differences appear. The SES coefficient (b) and explained rent variance, R^2, both differ across models.

SES variables explain anywhere from 18.7% to 20.2% of the rent variation. R^2 values decline slightly as bigger and bigger jumps in status are represented by a one-unit change in the SES variable.

The three different constants, or intercepts, reference different properties depending on the model. In Model 1, the constant ($133.94) references average predicted rent for the first property, Mediterranean Avenue, at various development levels. In Model 2, the constant ($140.16) references average predicted rent for properties in the first color sequence, Mediterranean and Baltic, again, averaged across development levels. In Model 3, the constant ($197.98) references average predicted rent for all properties on the first side of the board averaged across stages of development.

Predicted increases in rent associated with a one-unit increase in SES are as follows: $31.92 if moving up one property, $93.97 if moving up one color, and $180.72 if moving up one side of the board. Since this is a linear model, these are *average* increases for each additional unit increase on the predictor.

Next Step

Adapt the program to run these same regressions for the inflation-adjusted rent variable, `rent2022`.

Note

1 Not discussed here, the do file also generates residual and predicted scores.

5 Monolevel Models Part II

One-way Analysis of Variance (ANOVA)

Purpose

At heart, the simplest multilevel model is a one-way analysis of variance (ANOVA). The monolevel regression model in the last chapter predicted rent using SES variables that ordered the different groups of properties. The monolevel ANOVA in this chapter uses unordered groupings. Appreciating how monolevel ANOVA models work paves the way for understanding multilevel ANOVA models.

Chapter 4's regression models focus on explained versus residual rent variation. The ANOVA model here, instead, contrasts rent variation arising from average differences *between* groups with rent differences arising *within* groups. The groups considered here are the four neighborhood groupings, the four sides of the playing board.

Buckets of Unexplained Outcome Variation Illustrate the "Where" Question

Figure 5.1 shows a bucket of unexplained outcome variation. Initially, it is filled with water, that is, unexplained variation in rent. After using SES predictors to explain rent, the water level (unexplained variation) goes down, about 18–20%. That is the amount removed from the bucket, or explained away, as shown by the results in Table 4.1. This is how monolevel modelers think about the "Where is the outcome variation?" question. There is just one bucket, and water, or unexplained outcome variation, is removed as predictors are added. As R^2 goes up, unexplained outcome variation ($1 - R^2$, the coefficient of alienation) goes down.

Multilevel models, however, frame the question differently. A multilevel model with two levels – level-1 for individual rent values and level-2 for the groups into which the rent values and their properties are clustered – starts

DOI: 10.4324/9781003392682-5

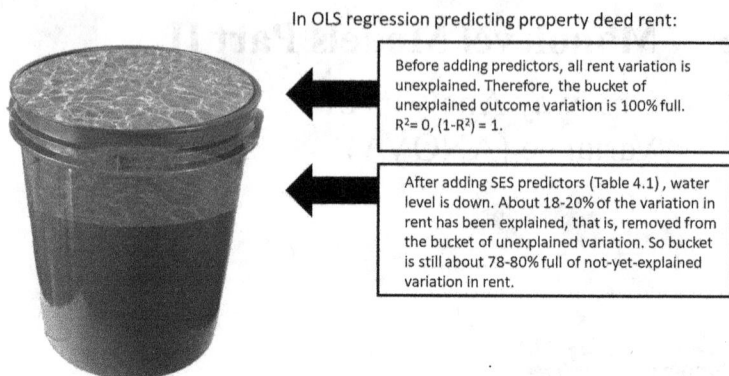

In OLS regression predicting property deed rent:

Before adding predictors, all rent variation is unexplained. Therefore, the bucket of unexplained outcome variation is 100% full. $R^2 = 0$, $(1-R^2) = 1$.

After adding SES predictors (Table 4.1), water level is down. About 18-20% of the variation in rent has been explained, that is, removed from the bucket of unexplained variation. So bucket is still about 78-80% full of not-yet-explained variation in rent.

Figure 5.1   Bucket of unexplained outcome variation, before and after OLS regressions using different SES variables.

with two different buckets, each completely full of water, that is, unexplained outcome variation. Together, the two buckets hold 100% of the total not-yet-explained outcome variation.

The multilevel models *assume* that the unexplained outcome variation *may arise from processes taking place at multiple levels*. Consider the running Monopoly example. Individual rent differences arise from level-1 real estate development dynamics. The latter are reflected in the presence of guesthouses and hotels. At level 2, average rent differences across the four sides arise from SES stratification as one moves around the playing board. Figure 5.2 depicts how the multilevel modeler conceptually frames "Where is the outcome variation?"

The question mark in the figure reflects the situation before the multi-level modeler has collected any empirical evidence. The modeler *assumes* that dynamics operating at two levels, level 1 and level 2, could *both* drive outcome scores.

Of course, that assumption needs testing. Perhaps the level-2 or group-level dynamics are not relevant; the group dynamics could be so weak that their influence is indistinguishable from random noise in the data. If so, then level-2 dynamics could be ignored and a monolevel model deployed.

Alternatively, group-level dynamics could deserve attention. If so, a multilevel model is needed, and the next question is as follows. How strong are those group-level dynamics? That is, how big should the level-2 bucket be relative to the level-1 bucket if, initially, both buckets are full to the

Figure 5.2 Before starting analyses, a multilevel modeler assumes scores could be driven by processes at multiple levels. Thus 100% of the outcome variations arises from two different buckets of variation. Before analyses begin, each is completely filled with unexplained outcome variation. The initial question is, what is the relative size of each bucket? In other words, how much does each bucket contribute to total outcome variation?

brim of unexplained outcome variation? Should the two buckets be the same size, as shown here, implying that group dynamics contribute 50% to the total outcome variation? Alternatively, should the level-2 bucket be much smaller?

Focusing now just on results when rents are grouped by four neighborhoods, results from the last chapter (Table 4.1: Model 3) provide a preliminary answer. Neighborhood SES differences explained 18.7% of the variance in rent. If the neighborhood SES ordering *explained* that much rent variation, the initial group-level *un*explained rent variation must have been at least that amount.

That initial estimate of level 2 rent variation, however, might be too low. The neighborhood SES variable used for the four sides of the board may not have captured all the group rent differences. Sidezero orders the four sides of the board (0, 1, 2, 3). OLS regression is a linear model, modeling a linear impact of sidezero on rent. In other words, each change in the predictor score is estimated to affect rent the same way. A change in predictor value from 0 to 1 was estimated to have the same rent impact as going from 1 to 2. This approach may be incomplete. Therefore, to get a more precise monolevel estimate of between-neighborhood rent variation, one needs the following: an analysis considering all the group differences and allowing any size rent differences between any pair of neighborhoods.

Structure of the Chapter

One-way or simple analysis of variance meets this need. It asks, considering the entire set of groups at once: is the *amount of outcome variation associated with differences in the set of group-level rent means more than just noise in the data?* Reviewing this model will help clarify random intercepts in multilevel models. The full set of 132 rent values, grouped by the four different sides of the board, are analyzed. Investigation centers on these questions:

- When rents are separated by the four SES levels on different sides of the playing board, do mean rents, as a set, differ significantly from one another?
- What fraction of rent variation in the outcome arises from these between-group differences? Stated differently, how much of the variation in rent goes in the group-level-differences bucket? The remainder necessarily goes in the within-group bucket.
- Which specific neighborhood mean rents differ significantly from which other ones?

These questions are revisited in the next chapter using a multilevel rather than a monolevel one-way ANOVA model.

One-way Analysis of Variance

Does Not Care About the Level of Measurement Used to Separate Predictor Groups

A one-way analysis of variance (ANOVA) makes no assumptions about relationships between groups determined by the predictor variable. Stated more formally, the level of measurement for the predictor variable defining each group could be nominal, ordinal, interval, or ratio; it does not matter. Usually, there are at least three different groups.[1] The categorization of cases into groups must be both mutually exclusive and exhaustive.

Assumptions of ANOVA

Analysis of variance makes many statistical assumptions.

1) "We shall have to assume normality" of the outcome variable (Blalock, 1979, p. 336).
2) "Independent random samples" (Blalock, 1979). Although there is no sampling here, the four groups on different sides of the board are independent. For example, there has been no matching across groups.
3) "Equal population standard deviations" (Blalock, 1979, p. 336); in regression terms, this is the assumption of homoscedasticity of variance, roughly comparable outcome variances across the level-2 groups.

4) In the full population of records from which random samples were drawn, one assumes "the null hypothesis," which is that "the population means [on the outcome variable] are equal" (Blalock, 1979, p. 336). Of course, the modeler seeks to reject this last assumption under the logic of null hypothesis significance testing. Since the dataset is the population of records, not a sample, the last assumption can be restated as follows: mean rent differences across the four sides of the playing board are indistinguishable from chance or random differences.

Using Neighborhood Differences to Predict Rent

Visual Examination

Figure 5.3 plots the rent distribution separately for each neighborhood. Reflecting the stratification by SES built in by game designers, median rents increase as one progresses around the board. Wider interquartile ranges as one progresses suggest unequal rather than roughly equal variances, signaling a heteroscedasticity problem.

Descriptive Statistics by Group

Table 5.1 presents descriptive statistics for rent, separately for each neighborhood. Going from the first to the second side of the board, rent for an average property in an average stage of development – between two and three

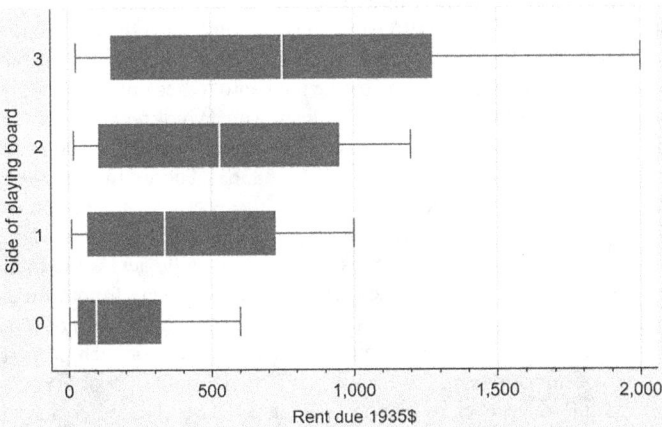

Figure 5.3 Separate box-and-whisker plots showing the distribution of the rent variable separately by sides of the playing board.

Table 5.1 Descriptive statistics for rent, by side of board

Statistic	Side of Board			
	0	1	2	3
N	30	36	36	30
Min	$2	$10	$18	$26
Max	$600	$1,000	$1,200	$2,000
Mean	$192.2	$394.6	$542.1	$747.7
Median	$95	$335	$530	$750
Variance	$37.356	$114.914	$183.882	$350.709
Standard Deviation	$193.3	$339	$428.8	$592.2

Note: Variance and standard deviation values on each side of the board reflect within-group variation.

guesthouses – more than doubles, going from $192 to $395. Going from the first to the third side of the board, the average price change is slightly less than a tripling, rising from $192 to $542. Going from the first to the fourth side of board, average rent nearly quadruples, from $192 to $748.

Behind the Scenes: Separating Variation on Rent Into Two Different Buckets

The one-way ANOVA approaches the problem differently than OLS regression. (1) Most importantly, the one-way ANOVA, unlike the regression model in the last chapter, divides unexplained outcome variation into two buckets: between-group (bucket on the right, Figure 5.2) and within-group (bucket on the left, Figure 5.2). (2) ANOVA works with "variation (as distinct from variance) [which] refer[s] to the sum of the squared deviations from the mean . . . a sum of squares, without dividing by the number of cases involved" (Blalock, 1979, p. 338). (3) ANOVA works not by testing mean differences but rather by "making two independent estimates of the common variance" and considering the ratio between the two (Blalock, 1979, p. 336).[2] These "two independent estimates" will determine the size of the two buckets for rent variation.

The first bucket (Figure 5.2, on the right) fills with outcome variation reflecting differences between groups. More specifically, across the four different sides of the board, how much rent variation is arising from differences between the *overall mean*, $469, and the *mean rents on each side of the board*?

Figure 5.4 shows the distribution of individual rents, for each property at each stage of development, for each of the four sides of the board. The solid horizontal line references overall mean rent, $469.06. The other horizontal lines reference mean rents for each side of the board. Each vertical arrow shows the discrepancy between that group's mean rent and overall mean rent. For sidezero = 1, grouping properties from St. Charles Place to New York Avenue, average rent ($394.61) is slightly below the overall mean ($469.06).

For sidezero = 2, grouping properties from Kentucky Avenue to Marvin Gardens, average rent ($542.06) is slightly above the overall mean. Moving to more extreme discrepancies, for sidezero = 0, grouping Mediterranean to Connecticut Avenues, average rent ($192.20) is substantially below the overall average. Finally, for sidezero = 3, grouping Pacific Avenue to Boardwalk, mean rent ($747.67) is substantially above overall mean rent.

Calculating the Between-Group Sum of Squares

If we

- for each arrow in Figure 5.4,
- took the difference between the rent value corresponding to the top of the arrow and the rent value corresponding to the bottom of the arrow – that is, the difference between the respective group mean and the overall mean,
- then squared each difference,
- then multiplied that squared difference by the number of cases in each group so that groups containing more records counted more,
- then added up this up across the four groups, that is, summed up the squared terms, the result would be the variation in rent associated with the group deviations from the grand mean.

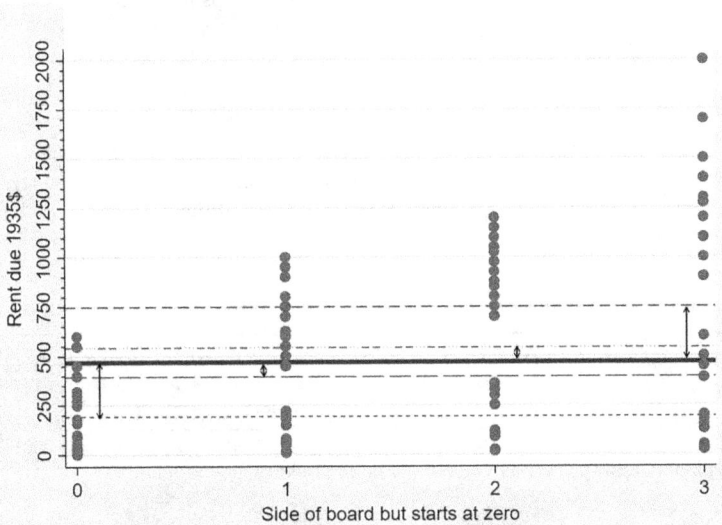

Figure 5.4 Four sources of between-group variation in rent across 132 rent values. The solid black horizontal line represents overall mean rent. Other horizontal lines reference mean rent values for four different sides of the board. Vertical arrows show the distances between each group mean and the overall mean.

This is the between-group variation in rent. It is just a number, albeit a rather large one, a bit over five million dollars: $5,019,549.60. This describes how much of the variation in rent arises from the differences in mean rent across the four sides of the board. This sum of squared differences controls for varying numbers of records in each group by multiplying the discrepancy between the group mean and the overall mean by the number of cases in each group.

Here is where to find it in output. After the command `oneway rent sidezero`, it appears in the analysis of variance table under the column "SS," for the source row "Between groups." After the command `regress rent i.sidezero` it appears in the top ANOVA table in the column labeled "SS" and the "Source" row labeled "Model." It also appears in Table 5.2.

The analysis also controls for the number of different groups analyzed. It divides the between-group sum of squared differences by the degrees of freedom (df) associated with the groups. The degrees of freedom for the grouping variable equal the number of groups minus one ($j-1$; here, $4-1=3$). Dividing model sum of squares by the number of groups minus 1 generates the mean sum of squared differences associated with the model ($1,673,183.20). The model is just that groups differ on average rent. This is also an estimate of the between-group rent variance. It is in the MS column.

In short, in calculating the sum of squared differences associated with the model of average rent differences across the four groups, one controls at various points both for the number of sampled addresses at different development stages in each group and for the total number of groups investigated.

The Signal: The Numerator in the F test as an Indicator of Predictor Impact

The mean squared difference, the $1.67 million figure noted previously, is what the F test uses as the numerator when calculating group impact on rent. This is the signal associated with mean group rent differences. The number

Table 5.2 One-way analysis of variance predicting rent

	SS (Sum of squared differences)	df	MS (Mean squared difference = Estimate of variance)	F	Prob > F
Between groups	$5,019,549.60	3	$1,673,183.20	9.86	< .0001
Within groups	$21,711,769.90	128	$169,623.20		
Total	$26,731,319.50	131	$204,055.87		

Note: Portion of one-way ANOVA output. Grouping variable = four sides of playing board (`sidezero`).

captures *the average effect* of different group memberships on the outcome variable, where "effect" references the average group-level mean rent discrepancy from overall average rent.

The Noise in the Data: The Denominator in the F Test Captures
Within-Group Variation

Every test of statistical inference examines a ratio of signal/noise, or impact/uncertainty. In the numerator of the F test, the signal is the average rent-discrepancy-creating effect of group membership, the $1.67 million. In the denominator is the noise in the data. Relevant numbers appear in the "within groups" row in Table 5.2. The total noise or uncertainty, the $21.7 million figure in this row, is a pooled estimate of within-group variation on rent.

This estimate is built on a record-by-record basis. See Figure 5.5, which shows how Boardwalk with a hotel contributes to this figure. The rent, $2,000, is $1,252.33 higher than the average rent, $747.67, in *that* neighborhood. For each side of the board, rent discrepancies, like this one, across all the properties in the neighborhood at all stages of development, capture within-group

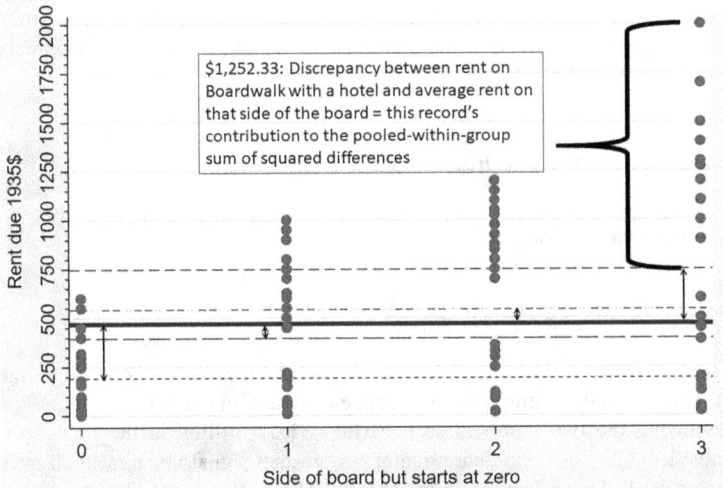

Figure 5.5 The height of the bracket indicates the size of the discrepancy between the rent for Boardwalk with a hotel and the average rent on the fourth side of the board; it is the contribution of this property at this stage of development to within-group variation in rent.

rent variation. That number is then pooled, or added up, across four sides of the board.

The steps to get *pooled within-group sum of squared differences* are these:

- Take each record,
- Subtract the corresponding group mean to get a (record – group) difference,
- Square that difference,
- Add up all those squared differences for the records in that group,
- Proceed to the next group ... the next ... and the next ... until all groups have been considered, and
- Add up all these within-group squared differences across all the groups.

These differences are not differences from the overall mean but rather differences between each record and its respective group mean. The total value is $21,711,769.90.

To get a mean estimate, which is a mean within-group variance estimate, divide this number by the degrees of freedom (df) associated with this pooled within-group variation. df = [number of cases – 1 = 131] – [number of groups – 1 = 3] = 128).

Dividing the sum by the df = $21,711,769.90/128 = $169,623.20.

This value, $169,623.20, can be viewed two ways. (1) It is an estimate of within-group variance in rent. (2) It is an estimate of the squared within-group rent discrepancy for an average property at an average stage of development in an average neighborhood.

Checking Against a One-Way ANOVA

Run a one-way analysis of variance (oneway rent sidezero) to confirm these calculations.

The Impact/Noise Ratio: The F Test

The F test or F ratio compares the between-group variance estimate, in the numerator, to the within-group variance estimate, in the denominator.[3] Just reviewing the two numbers seen earlier, $1.67 million in the numerator and $169,623.20 in the denominator, suggests a signal/noise ratio slightly under 10:1. The F-test value is actually 9.86 (Table 5.2). The associated probability value of an F-test value this high or higher with 3 and 128 df_1 *and df_2* is less than one in 10,000 (p < .0001). Conclude as follows: the chances of getting neighborhood mean rent differences this big or bigger just because of random groupings in the data are less than about one in 10,000. Mean rent differences across the four sides of the board are more than random noise.

Using Sums of Squares Separated Into Two Buckets to get to Explained Variance: R^2

Return to the sum of squared differences already partitioned in Table 5.2 into two buckets: one for differences between four neighborhood groups, the other for the pooled within-group variation (Table 5.2). Those two sources comprise the total variation in rent. Roughly, about $5 million of the sum of squared differences comes from between group differences, and about $22 million comes from within-group differences. These add up to almost $27 million in sums of squared differences. Five compared to 27 is a bit less than a fifth.

These numbers can generate explained variance or R^2. Calculating the between-group sum of squares as a percentage of the total sum of squares:

$$\frac{\$5,019,550 \; (\text{Between group SS})}{\$26,731,320 \; (\text{Total SS})} \; \text{Ratio} = 0.188$$

The between-group variation is 18.8% of the total rent variation. This is also R^2. The F test argues this amount arose from more than just random group differences.

This answers the question posed earlier. If rents are grouped by neighborhoods, the four sides of the playing board, in a manner capturing *all* of the group rent differences, those group differences make up 18.8% of all the variation in rents.

The Bartlett Test

One line of output not yet discussed is this:

Bartlett's equal-variances test: $\chi^2(3) = 33.1820$ Prob $> \chi^2 = 0.000$

By default, Stata tests the assumption of homoscedasticity, that within-group rent variances are roughly equal across the different groups. Figure 5.3 showed markedly different interquartile ranges across the different sides of the playing board. Now, the Bartlett test confirms statistically that the equal group variance assumption of the F test has not been met. The null hypothesis of the Bartlett test is that group variances are equal. The significant chi-squared (χ^2) test ($p < .001$) rejects the equal variances assumption.

Group rent variances are heteroscedastic, not homoscedastic. With a "real" F test with "real" data, we might do something about this.[4] Doing something could involve transforming the outcome variable. That matter is taken up in Chapter 8.

Going Further: Significant Pairwise Neighborhood Mean Rent Differences

The one-way ANOVA results simply say this: as a set, these four groups differ significantly on average rent. Not yet answered, however, is which specific groups differ significantly from which other specific groups on average rent? The answer requires post-estimation or post hoc tests. Many are available. Each controls for the number of pairs of group means being compared.[5]

Here, the Scheffé (1959) post hoc test is used. The Stata command is:

```
oneway rent sidezero, tabulate Scheffe
```

The Scheffé post hoc results in Table 5.3 show pairwise group mean differences using row and column combinations. For example, the first entry in the upper left says there's a difference of $202.41 ($394.61 − $192.20) in average rent between the first side of the board after "GO" (sidezero = 0) and the second side of the board (sidezero = 1). The probability value (p = .272) says the mean rent difference between these

Table 5.3 Scheffé post hoc pairwise comparison tests

Column group	Row group		
	0	1	2
1	$202.41 (0.272)		
2	$349.86 (0.01)	$147.44 (0.513)	
3	$555.47 (<.001)	$353.06 (0.009)	$205.61 (0.258)

Note: Entries = [Row mean – Column mean] Statistical significance of the group mean difference in parentheses. The four neighborhoods are referenced by the sidezero variable, which starts at 0 for the first side of the playing board after "GO" and ends at 3 for the fourth side of the playing board.

two neighborhoods *could* have arisen simply from random groupings of records into these two groups. This statistical indistinguishability of mean rents applies as well for the other two pairwise comparisons of adjacent groups ($p = .513$ and $p = .258$).

These results shed light on how Parker Brothers' game developers arranged the game. Statistically speaking – that is, in the long run – mean rent differences between two adjacent sides of the board could be arising just from random noise. To see a significant difference in average rents requires contrasting averages from non-adjacent neighborhoods on the playing board.

Checking Your One-Way Analysis of Variance With a Regression Model

Run the same one-way ANOVA using a regression model. It provides additional details.

Doing the Same Thing "On the Fly" With a Regression Model

Do this "on the fly." Put `i.` in front of the `sidezero` variable in the regression command:

```
regress rent i.sidezero
```

Stata turns the predictor into three separate dummy variables, leaving out the lowest-scoring group, the first side of the board, as the reference string. This is also called a *factor variable*, a categorical variable converted to a set of indicator variables. See Table 5.4.

Table 5.4 Coding of dummy variables created by converting sidezero variable into a set of indicator variables

Sidezero score	Indicator variable name in Stata output		
	Sidezero_1	Sidezero_2	Sidezero_3
0 (Mediterranean Avenue to Connecticut Avenue)	0	0	0
1 (St. Charles Place to New York Avenue)	1	0	0
2 (Kentucky Avenue to Marvin Gardens)	0	1	0
3 (Pacific Avenue to Boardwalk)	0	0	1

Note: Invoking `i.sidezero` rather than `sidezero` in the regression command turns the ordinal variable into three separate indicator or dummy variables. Each dummy variable contrasts the specified group with the reference string, Mediterranean to Connecticut Avenues. The reference string is coded 0 on all the dummy variables.

Regression results appear in Figure 5.6. *These* results are different from those using the `sidezero` variable that scores 0,1,2,3 (Table 4.1, Model 3). *That* regression with the `sidezero` variable generated just *one* coefficient (b = $180.72) indicating the impact of *increasing one unit* on the predictor, for example going from the first side of the board to the second side of the board. The underlying assumption in Table 4.1, Model 3, was that an increase of one unit on `sidezero` meant the same thing, regardless of playing board position. In other words, a constant linear impact on rent was assumed for progressing from one side of the board to the next.

In Figure 5.6, three different b weights, and the associated t tests of significance, describe the estimated difference between average rent on the first side of the board versus the second ($202.41), on the first versus the third side ($349.86), and on the first versus the fourth side ($555.47). The constant ($192.20) captures estimated average rent for the first side of the board.

Look closely. The b weight for `sidezero_2` is *not* twice the b weight of `sidezero_1`. The b weight for `sidezero_3` is *not* three times the b weight for `sidezero_1`. This demonstrates that, as one progresses around the board, the rent impact of moving up one neighborhood is not precisely linear.

A term in this table that might be new is MSE, for mean square error. It is an indicator of unexplained variation, analogous to but different from the coefficient of alienation ($1 - R^2$). To calculate MSE, each residual (observed–predicted) value for each record is squared, the numbers are added up, and the sum divided by the number of observations. The value is a record-level indicator of average squared error associated with this regression model.

```
. regress rent i.sidezero
```

Source	SS	df	MS		Number of obs	=	132
					F(3, 128)	=	9.86
Model	5019549.6	3	1673183.2		Prob > F	=	0.0000
Residual	21711769.9	128	169623.202		R-squared	=	0.1878
					Adj R-squared	=	0.1687
Total	26731319.5	131	204055.874		Root MSE	=	411.85

rent	Coefficient	Std. err.	t	P>|t|	[95% conf. interval]	
sidezero						
1	202.4111	101.8129	1.99	0.049	.9569349	403.8653
2	349.8556	101.8129	3.44	0.001	148.4014	551.3097
3	555.4667	106.3401	5.22	0.000	345.0546	765.8787
_cons	192.2	75.19379	2.56	0.012	43.41623	340.9838

Figure 5.6 Stata output: regression results predicting rent with three categorical variables representing different sides of the playing board.

What Is the Same: Comparing ANOVA and Regression

Compare ANOVA results, including post hoc Scheffé pairwise comparison tests, to regression results with the factor variable (Figure 5.6). Several things are the same:

- F test of the R^2
- R^2, although getting it from the ANOVA table requires running some numbers
- Sums of squared differences total
- Sums of squared differences between groups (also called model)
- Sums of squared differences within groups (also called residual)
- Mean difference values between the first group and each of the other three groups. These are the b weights appearing in the regression table (Figure 5.6), and these correspond to the differences in the first column of the Scheffé post hoc test table (Table 5.3).

What Is Different: Comparing ANOVA and Regression

Nonetheless, there are differences. The p values associated with the t tests in the regression output (Figure 5.6) contrast average predicted rents in the second through fourth sides with average predicted rent for the first side. These correspond to the first column of Scheffé post hoc tests (Table 5.3). The b weights are the same, but some significance levels differ. For example, comparing mean rent differences between the first versus second side, the Scheffé test says the $202 difference is non-significant ($p = .272$), while the t test of the b weight finds significance ($p = .049$).

Why the discrepancy? Several factors contribute (Keselman & Rogan, 1978, p. 48). (1) The Scheffé procedure is a multiple-comparison procedure. (2) Although it uses a t test like the t test of the b weight, the Scheffé test defines the variances for the denominator in the test differently. (3) The Scheffé test derives critical values for determining significance differently (Keselman & Rogan, 1978, Eq. 2.5b).

Which approach to follow? It depends on the purpose. The ANOVA followed by the post hoc Scheffé test informs about the entire *set* of pairwise mean differences. Dummy variable regression only compares differences between the first side of the board, the reference string, and each of the other three sides.

Back to the Buckets and Looking Ahead

Remember the buckets question: "Where is the rent variation?" Two monolevel procedures have provided the same answer. See Figure 5.7. The

Figure 5.7 Multilevel model view of ANOVA and regression models predicting side-of-board differences in average rent.

unexplained between-group rent variation bucket holds 18.78% of the total unexplained variation.

A monolevel modeler would say at this point that neighborhood differences explain 18.78% of the variation in rent (Figure 5.1). A multilevel modeler would frame it differently (Figure 5.7): (1) There is some, as yet unspecified, group-level process driving neighborhood mean rent differences because the *F* test of the R^2 says the level-2 variation is more than noise. (2) These neighborhood-level dynamics are driving 18.78% of the rent differences.

The multilevel modeler, moreover, poses additional questions:

(3) Do these group differences remain important if each neighborhood mean rent value is adjusted based on features of the entire *set* of group means? Such adjustments are carried out using empirical Bayes estimation. See Chapter 6.
(4) Can the between-group mean rent differences be accounted for by within-group features – that is, level-1 variables? See Chapter 7.
(5) What specific level-2 variables contribute to group differences? See Chapter 10.

Notes

1 With only two groups, a *t* test for a normally distributed outcome or a test of proportions for a binary outcome would suffice.
2 "One of these estimates . . . will be a weighted average of the [outcome] variances *within* each of the separate samples [or groups] . . . each sample [or group] variance

will be computed separately and will involve only the deviation from the mean of that particular sample [or group] . . . the second estimate of the common variance involves the variance of the separate sample [or group] means treated as individual scores . . . the deviations of the sample [or group] means about the grand mean will be used . . . the test used in analysis of variance involves a comparison of the two separate estimates . . . we take the ratio of the second estimate to the first" to calculate the F test (Blalock, 1979, pp. 336–338).

3 Where does the name "F test" come from? No, it is not because tests A–E failed. The analysis of variance was developed in the early 20th century by British statistician Sir Ronald Fisher. Another statistician, G. W. Snedecor, in his 1937 statistics textbook *Statistical Methods Applied to Experiments in Agriculture and Biology* (1st ed., Iowa State College Press), proposed the name "F test" in honor of Fisher (Mainland, 1954).

4 How successfully the F test can cope with such violations, and what alternate tests might be preferred, is an ongoing area of scholarly work (Lachenbruch & Clements, 1991).

5 Following an F test, *always* run these post hoc tests rather than a series of t tests. The latter fail to control for the number of simultaneous post hoc comparisons, which may result in inflated α levels and therefore inflated experiment-wise Type I error rates.

6   First Multilevel Model

No Predictors

Purpose

This chapter introduces the simplest multilevel model. It goes by various names: the null model, the unconditional model, the ANOVA model, and the random intercepts model. It is called the "null" or "unconditional" model because it has no predictors. "The simplest possible hierarchical linear model is equivalent to a one-way ANOVA with random effects" (Raudenbush & Bryk, 2002, p. 23). This model is testing one big idea with two parts:

(1) Do groups vary significantly on the outcome, after adjusting level-2 group means? And if they do,
(2) How much of the variation in the outcome is associated with these adjusted group differences?

The terms "adjusted," "adjusting," and "adjustments" involve empirical Bayes (EB) adjustments, covered later in the chapter. This is something new.
    This chapter covers the following:

1. How multilevel models extend the one-way ANOVA model (Table 5.2, Figure 5.6);
2. What resulting parameters represent;
3. How to examine group outcome differences;
4. How to decide whether a multilevel model is needed;
5. What empirical Bayes (EB) adjustments are doing to the data and why; and
6. How the model handles errors in a different way.

Equation alert! This chapter contains equations. These help formally summarize model operations. I will go slowly when introducing each one. If you go slowly too, you will understand more fully what is afoot.

DOI: 10.4324/9781003392682-6

The Bucket Problem

Let's consider the buckets question (Chapter 5) but in a slightly different way: after making empirical Bayes (EB) adjustments to neighborhood average rents. The purpose of the investigation remains the same.

- Descriptively, how big is the variation in average rents across the four sides of the board, the four neighborhoods?
- Are these group-level differences in average neighborhood rents more than noise in the data?

Equations

In the multilevel model considered here, individual rent values are the level-1 units, and the four sides of the board are the level-2 groups.

The Level-1 Equation

Recall a basic regression equation (Table 4.1, Model 3) predicting rent with one neighborhood SES predictor (X_1):

$$Y(rent) = a + \beta_1 X_1 + e \qquad \text{(Eq. 6.1)}$$

Now taking away the predictor, $X1$, and its associated β weight, leaves this equation:

$$Y = a + e \qquad \text{(Eq. 6.2)}$$

Where:
- a = the constant; also the overall or grand mean on rent
- e = the error or deviation of each individual rent value from rent's grand mean

Now, to translate this last equation into a multilevel model format. These models use a different letter and a specific subscript to capture the constant. Instead of a, a Greek uppercase beta (β) and a 0 subscript appears; call it "b naught" or "beta naught." Also, substitute the letter r for residual instead of e for the error. So now, the equation looks like this.

$$Y = \beta_0 + r \qquad \text{(Eq. 6.3)}$$

If and only if data are monolevel, not grouped, Eq. 6.3 would mean the same thing as Eq. 6.2. It would describe all the data. If the data *are multilevel,* however, and if that grouping is reflected in the model, the equation needs modification. It needs to reflect the situation for records *within* a particular level-2 group. In short, it needs to be transformed into a depiction of the level-1 relationship. This is done by adding subscripts. By convention:

Subscript *i*   refers to observations 1 . . . *n* for each level-1 unit within
                    each level-2 group
Subscript *j*   refers to level-2 groups 1 . . . *j*

With subscripts, Eq. 6.4 forms the level-1 equation for the ANOVA multilevel model:

$$Y_{ij} = \beta_{0j} + r_{ij}$$ (Eq. 6.4, the level-1 equation[1])

Where:
- β_{0j} = mean rent after adjustments for each group (each side of board), 1 through *j* (4);
- r_{ij} = the deviation in rent between record *i* in group *j*, and the adjusted mean rent for that group.

The typical formula for a residual is $Y_{residual} = (Y_{observed} - Y_{predicted})$. Subtracting β_{0j} from each side of Eq. 6.4 now describes level-1 residuals: $r_{ij} = (Y_{ij} - \beta_{0j})$.

Note the following new idea. The new term β_{0j} (Eq. 6.4), because it has a *j* subscript, means that *each* group – here, *each* side of the playing board – could have its *own* average outcome score.

But do we "need" to allow each group to have its own average? Is this introducing an unnecessary complexity? Perhaps one group mean is sufficient for all the different groups? The level-2 equation structures this question in a specific way.

The Level-2 Equation

The level-2 equation for the ANOVA multilevel model describes the average neighborhood rents for each side of the board. This contrasts with the level-1 equation that predicts individual rent values in relation to each group's average rent value.

The level-2 equation, however, links to the level-1 equation. Specifically, the former predicts a result generated by the latter: the β_{0j} estimated parameter values. The level-2 equation is predicting a level-1 model feature, not a data feature.

This leads to another big idea in mixed-effects modeling. In a two-level model, parameters estimated on the prediction side in a level-1 equation have corresponding level-2 equations where each is an outcome. Consequently there can be *multiple* level-2 equations if the corresponding level-1 equation generates multiple parameters.

Further, this process applies for models with more than two levels. For example, individual residents (level 1) reporting personal safety concerns might be nested within different neighborhoods (level 2), which in turn might be nested within different cities (level 3). Not only could we take features of the level-1 equations and predict them with level-2 equations. We also could take features of the level-2 equations and in turn try to predict them with level-3 equations.

Only One Value for All the Different Groups?

There are different ways to write the level-2 equation predicting adjusted neighborhood average rent values, the β_{0j} values. One way allows only *one* value:

$$\beta_{0j} = \gamma_{00} \qquad\qquad (\text{Eq. } 6.5^2)$$

Where:
- β_{0j} = mean average outcome score (here, average rent) in each group (here, each side of the board), after EB adjustments.
- γ_{00} [pronounced "gamma naught naught"] = overall average outcome score, here, average rent, for all records, all sides of the board, after adjustments.

Read this as "Beta naught j equals gamma naught naught."

Conceptually this equation says the following. Mean rent values for all four neighborhoods essentially have just one value. Variation around that one value is just random noise. Therefore, just one value in the model (γ_{00}) adequately captures group means on rent. That one value is the grand mean – after some adjustments – for all rent values, all properties, in all neighborhoods, at all stages of development. In ANOVA terminology, this asserts the null hypothesis of no significant difference across groups on average rent values.

Different Values Needed for Different Group?

A second way of writing the level-2 equation allows multiple values, as follows:

$$\beta_{0j} = \gamma_{00} + u_{0j} \qquad\qquad (\text{Eq. } 6.6)$$

Where:

- β_{0j} = mean outcome score (here, average rent) in each group $1 \ldots j$ (here, each side of the board) after adjustments.
- γ_{00} = overall average outcome score (here, average rent) in the entire set of records, after adjustments
- u_{0j} ["u naught j"; this is just the letter u, not the Greek letter mu (μ)] = the discrepancy between group j's mean outcome score – here, adjusted mean rent on each side of the board – and the overall adjusted mean outcome score for all the records for all the groups.[3] Level-2 discrepancies are "assumed to have a mean of zero and variance τ_{00} [pronounced 'tau naught naught']" (Raudenbush & Bryk, 2002, p. 24). Stated differently, u_{0j} is each group's adjusted *deviation* from the overall adjusted outcome score. Four neighborhood groups generate four different u_{0j} values.

The equation says each group's estimated average rent, its intercept or constant (β_{0j}), equals the estimated overall mean rent, after precision weighting (γ_{00}), plus that group's estimated deviation, after EB adjustments (u_{0j}), from the overall value.[4]

To unpack this new term, u_{0j}, see Figure 6.1. It shows the situation for just one group of level-1 observations: all rent values for all properties, at all stages of development, on the fourth side of the board, from Pacific Avenue to Boardwalk.

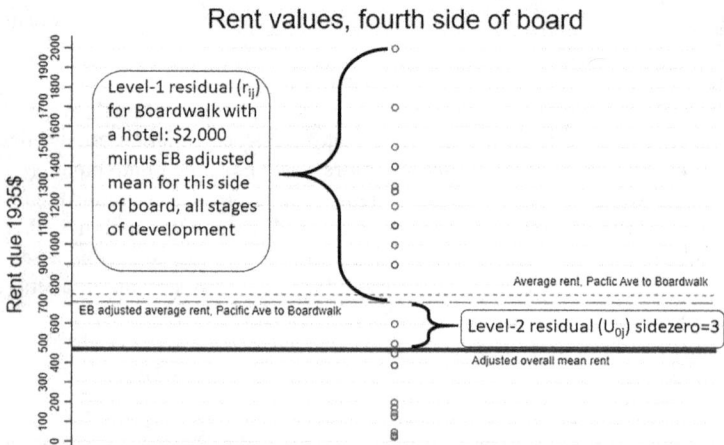

Figure 6.1 Rent values, fourth side of the board, for all properties, at all stages of development, along with the precision-weighted grand mean, average rent for this group of properties, and EB-adjusted average rent for this group of properties.

The three horizontal lines reference the following:

- Adjusted overall mean rent, $469.12 ($\gamma_{00,}$ solid line). This is for *all* properties, at *all* stages of development, on *all* sides of the board;
- Average neighborhood rent *just* for *this* neighborhood, the fourth side of the board, $747.67 (line with short dashes);
- EB-adjusted average neighborhood rent *just* for *this* neighborhood, the fourth side of the board, $709.18 (line with long dashes).

The level-2 residual for this group of rents (u_{04}) reflects the *discrepancy* between overall adjusted rent, $469.12 ($\gamma_{00}$), and the EB-adjusted average rent in this neighborhood, $709.18. The bracket opening toward the left in Figure 6.1 captures the size of that difference. More specifically, for this group of properties where $j = 4$, $u_{04} = \$709.18 - \$469.12 = \$240.06$.

Stated non-technically, after taking into account features of the entire dataset, rents for properties at different stages of development on the fourth side of the playing board had an estimated price, on average, $240.06 higher than the estimated average rent for all properties at all stages of development on all sides of the playing board.

Although only one group is shown here, more broadly, the level-2 equation is allowing each of the four neighborhoods to each have its own constant in the model, its own adjusted average rent. Therefore, for the fourth side of the board ($j = 4$) estimated adjusted mean rent is derived as follows:

$$\$709.18 \ (\beta_{04}) = \$469.12 \ (\gamma_{00}) + \$240.06 \ (u_{04})$$

Combining the Two Equations

One equation can describe both levels of this two-level multilevel model. Rearrange the level-1 equation (Eq. 6.4) to isolate β_{0j} ($\beta_{0j} = Y_{ij} - r_{ij}$), then substitute this into the level-2 equation (Eq. 6.6) so ($Y_{ij} - r_{ij} = \gamma_{00} + u_{0j}$).

Next, adding r_{ij} to each side of the equation produces one showing how each individual rent value is a function of something happening at both levels. The level-1 and level-2 combined model is

$$Y_{ij} = \gamma_{00} + u_{0j} + r_{ij} \qquad \text{(Raudenbush \& Bryk, 2002, p. 24, Eq. 2.8)}$$
$$\text{(Eq. 6.7)}$$

Equation 6.7 says each individual observed rent value (Y_{ij}) has three parts: the adjusted "grand mean" for rent (γ_{00}); plus "a group (level-2) effect" (u_{0j}) which is the EB adjusted neighborhood average rent discrepancy from the grand mean; plus an observation-level "(level-1) effect" (r_{ij}) which describes how rent observation i differs from the adjusted neighborhood average rent in its group j (Raudenbush & Bryk, 2002, p. 24). "It is a random effects model because the group effects are construed as random" (op cit).

Note that the combined level-1 plus level-2 formulation of the ANOVA multilevel model (Eq. 6.7) separates the residual, the error term (e) in a plain regression model, into two parts, one for each level. There is

- a between-group part (u_{0j}) capturing the mean deviation of the respective group from the overall average; and
- a within-group part (r_{ij}), capturing discrepancies between individual records and their adjusted group mean.

This same separation is illustrated in Figure 6.1, focusing just on the fourth side of the board.

Understanding Group Discrepancies as a Set

The adjusted group mean deviations from overall average rent, the u_{0j} values, are empirical Bayes (EB) estimates. These can be understood in different ways depending upon the data situation.

In the Monopoly® example, four groups ($j = 4$) represent four different sides of the board, four neighborhoods. The board has only four sides. The four sides were *not* sampled from some different board that had more than four sides. Consequently, the u_{0j} values "are fixed parameters . . . this is relevant if the groups j refer to categories each with their own distinct interpretation" (Snijders & Bosker, 2012, p. 45). This is the situation here. Other examples of groups that are distinct categories include different states in the US, different countries in the European Union, or the 12 different regional circuits of the US Courts of Appeals.

On the other hand, if data records represent a *sample* of level-2 units – for example, a sample of neighborhoods, a sample of organizations, a sample of cities, or a sample of persons each assessed multiple times – then the u_{0j} values represent "independent and identically distributed *random* variables" (Snijders & Bosker, 2012, p. 45).

Only in this second type of situation is a minimum number of level-2 units in the dataset advisable for multilevel modeling. A minimum number of level-2 units allows group deviations (u_{0j} values) to approximate a normal distribution of group means. To get that approximation, and for statistical power reasons as well, a minimum n of 50 to 80 level-2 units in your dataset is often recommended.[5]

Estimated Group Deviations Have a Variance

Since the level-2 equation (Eq. 6.6) allows each group its own adjusted mean outcome score and expresses those as deviations from the precision-weighted grand mean (γ_{00}), the set of multiple u_{0j} values will have a variance. The latter describes the amount of level-2 dispersion around the adjusted overall mean (γ_{00}).

Variance of u_{0j} values = τ_{00} (Tau, pronounced "taw [like "raw"]
naught naught")[6]   (Eq. 6.8)

Conceptually, and putting aside EB adjustments, in effect this is just a new name for the level-2 bucket filled with unexplained outcome variation (Figure 5.2, right-hand bucket). It is filled with τ_{00}.

Group Mean Variance Before Adjustments

Multilevel models make EB adjustments when calculating these group mean deviations from the overall outcome mean. How to get *closer* to this variation in group means, both before and after the means have been EB-adjusted? To start, get the variance of the group means ($Y.j$) *before* they are EB-adjusted.

1. Open the Monopoly dataset used in the last chapter.
2. Make a collapsed file with just four records, one for each neighborhood.
3. Collapse the rent variable by side of the board so there is a rent mean for each side of the board.
4. Save the overall mean in the collapsed file as well.
5. Subtract the overall mean from each group mean.
6. Save the collapsed file.
7. Using the collapsed file, request the descriptive statistic variance for the group-rent-discrepancies-from-overall-mean-by-side-of-board variable.
8. The value should be $55,048.03.

This is the variance of the four neighborhood-level mean discrepancies from overall rent, before any EB or precision-weighting adjustments.

Running the ANOVA Mixed Model, Interpreting Output

Running and Interpreting

To get the adjusted variance (τ_{00}) of the neighborhood rent averages, run the ANOVA multilevel model. Level-1 is individual rent values. Level-2 are the sides of the Monopoly board using the grouping variable sidezero which goes from 0 to 3. The first part of the results appears in Figure 6.2.[7]
Let's unpack output line by line.

147 The command mixed, followed by the outcome variable, followed by double pipes (||), then the level-2 grouping variable, and a colon. Stata output places a period in front of the command from the do file.

```
147  . mixed rent ||sidezero:
148
149  Performing EM optimization ...
150
151  Performing gradient-based optimization:
152  Iteration 0:    log likelihood =  -986.1665
153  Iteration 1:    log likelihood =  -986.1665
154
155  Computing standard errors ...
156
157  Mixed-effects ML regression          Number of obs     =      132
158  Group variable: sidezero             Number of groups  =        4
159                                       Obs per group:
160                                                    min =       30
161                                                    avg =     33.0
162                                                    max =       36
163                                       Wald chi2(0)      =        .
164  Log likelihood =  -986.1665          Prob > chi2       =        .
165
166  ------------------------------------------------------------------------------
167       rent | Coefficient  Std. err.     z    P>|z|   [95% conf. interval]
168  -------------+----------------------------------------------------------------
169      _cons |   469.124    100.5688    4.66   0.000    272.0127    666.2353
170  ------------------------------------------------------------------------------
171
172  ------------------------------------------------------------------------------
173  Random-effects parameters  |  Estimate   Std. err.   [95% conf. interval]
174  -------------------------------+----------------------------------------------
175  sidezero: Identity            |
176               var(_cons) |   35277.26    28910.56    7078.068    175822.7
177  -------------------------------+----------------------------------------------
178            var(Residual) |   169677.2    21216.5     132797.2    216799.4
179  ------------------------------------------------------------------------------
180  LR test vs. linear model: chibar2(01) = 15.11    Prob >= chibar2 = 0.0001
181
```

Figure 6.2 Results from the multilevel ANOVA model of rent for properties grouped by side of the playing board.

149 This is an iterative maximum likelihood estimation procedure, an expectation-maximization (EM) algorithm invented in the 1970s (Raudenbush & Bryk, 2002, p. 437). The analysis approximates a "best" solution after multiple attempts, stopping when the predicted data features closely match the observed data features, and additional adjustments in model parameters result in only minor improvements in matching. This type of estimation has implications for how we think about the mean group deviations produced.

151 The program will look for the optimal solution among many possible solutions.

152–153 An optimal solution surfaces after one iteration. There was a starting estimate (iteration 0), and then one reestimate, that is, one iteration (iteration 1). Each iteration has an associated log likelihood value (LL). The log likelihood value indicates the *lack of fit* between the proposed solution, that is, the estimated model, and the observed data. A *lower score indicates better fit*. Some programs generate a related statistic, deviance, which is [-2 * the LL value]. Note no change between iteration 0 and iteration 1 on this LL indicator of the lack of fit. That is why the algorithm stopped iterating. It could not do appreciably improve the initial estimate.[8]

155 It computes the accompanying standard errors of the "best" estimates.

157–164 Descriptive information appears: the type of model, mixed-effects maximum likelihood regression; the grouping variable, `sidezero`; the number of cases examined; the number of groups; and the minimum, maximum, and average number of observations per group.

Check descriptive information carefully; *under some types of models, some groups will be dropped from the analysis, but finding that this occurred requires careful checking.* The final LL value also is repeated. No value for the Wald chi-squared (χ^2) statistic appears because there are no predictors in the model, only the constants.

166–170 The analysis shows the *fixed-effects portion* of your model. This shows the impact of specific predictors.[9] The predictor in question here is just the constant (`_cons`), the precision-weighted overall rent average (γ_{00}): $469.12.[10]

You see the standard error associated with the overall mean ($100.57), and the upper and lower bounds of the 95% confidence interval around the constant: $666.24 to $272.01.

A z test of the overall average ($z = 4.66$; $p < .001$) appears.[11] It divides the constant by its standard error. This information is of no use unless you have a *specific reason* for testing the null hypothesis that the overall average score on the outcome is zero. I recommend routinely omitting this significance test of the constant unless testing a specific hypothesis.

172–179 This table shows the variance estimation portion of results with two variance estimates in the column "Estimate." Because just variances are reported here, this *portion* of the model is the *random effects portion* or the *varying effects portion.* What is varying are the adjusted neighborhood mean deviations (u_{0j} values) around overall rent.

176 var (`_cons`) = $35,277.26: variance ($\tau_{00}$), after adjustments, of the four adjusted group mean deviations on rent, that is, level-2, between-group outcome variance. This quantity fills up the level-2 between-group bucket (Figure 5.2). The variance estimate has an associated standard error ($28,910.56), and an upper (UCL) limit and lower limit (LCL) for its 95 percent confidence interval (UCL: $175,822.70; LCL: $7,078.07). If these data were from a representative probability sample, and the exact same sampling procedure was repeated 100 times, 95 times out of 100 the true population between-group variance would lie within this range, between these UCL and LCL values.

178 var (Residual) = $169,677.20: *pooled within-group outcome variance.* This quantity fills up with level-1, within-group bucket of outcome variation (Figure 5.2). It captures record-level squared discrepancies, within each group, between each record's rent and its respective

group-adjusted mean rent (u_{0j}), added up across all four groups. It also has an associated standard error ($21,216.50) and 95% confidence interval (UCL: $216,799.40; LCL: $132,797.20). Again, if these were data from a probability sample, and the sampling protocol was repeated 100 times, 95 times out of 100 the true population within-group variance would lie within this range.

Finally! After adjusting for data features, we know the amount of outcome variation in each bucket! See Figure 6.3.

Alert readers will notice that the between-group outcome variance, $35,277.26, based on the adjusted group mean deviations, is much smaller than the variance statistic based on the raw group mean deviations ($55,048.03). Why the shrinkage? The answer is empirical Bayes adjustments.

180 Are four constants needed? That is, do model parameters generate a significantly better fit to observed data if the model includes a separate adjusted rent constant for each neighborhood? Stated formally, *can the null hypothesis that the between-group variance on the outcome is zero be rejected?* Or are the neighborhood mean differences no more than random noise in the data? This line provides an answer using a likelihood ratio (LR) χ^2 test of this null hypothesis.[12] The χ^2 value, 15.11, with one

Figure 6.3 Allocation of outcome variation, after empirical Bayes adjustment and precision weighting, into between-group and within-group buckets. Each bucket is "filled" with the unexplained amount of rent variation shown.

degree of freedom, is significant ($p < .001$). The significant χ^2 value says: this model, with one extra parameter capturing the variance arising from allowing each group to have its own outcome mean, provides a significantly better fit between the model estimates and the rent data than a model with just one overall mean for rent. Therefore, reject the null hypothesis and conclude that a multilevel model fits these data better than a monolevel regression model. Variation in average rent across the four sides of the board *is* more than random noise in the data.

Theoretical Implications

In the language of level-2 equations, rejecting the "just random noise" idea means discarding this idea:

$$\beta_{0j} = \gamma_{00}$$

in favor of this idea:

$$\beta_{0j} = \gamma_{00} + u_{0j}$$

Theoretical implications follow. The significant LR χ^2 test result suggests group-level processes are at work (Liska, 1990), driving these neighborhood differences.[13] *Always* pay attention to this LR χ^2 test from the ANOVA model.[14] This test answers the same question addressed by the F test in the monolevel one-way ANOVA. Now, an empirical rationale exists for doing a multilevel rather than monolevel model.

Pulling the Lens Back: Model Rationale

Getting the Between-Group Outcome Proportion

The descriptive counterpart to the LR χ^2 test in the ANOVA multilevel model is the ICC or intraclass correlation (ρ [rho] or r_{icc}).[15] It reflects between-group outcome variation as a percentage of all outcome variation after EB adjustments.

ρ = between-group variance/(between-group variance + within-group variance)   (Eq. 6.9)

Plugging in numbers:

$\$35,277.26/(\$35,277.26 + \$169,677.20) = 0.172$

Alternatively, ask Stata for the answer with this postestimation command: `estat icc`. Results are identical.

Finally! Another definitive answer to the buckets question, "Where is the variation?" Answer: 17.2% of rent differences arise from level-2 neighborhood differences.

Is the Proportion Important?

What to do with this? Is 17% between-group variation low? Or high? Or important? Ignorable? On the one hand, the number is just descriptive. This is how the Parker Brothers game designers "programmed" the rent variable, stratifying values across four sides of the game board. On the other hand, should we care? Is it a paltry amount? Suppose it was just 10 percent? Or 5 percent? Would it be ignorable then?

Some say yes, you can ignore between-group outcome variation when it is below a certain threshold percentage (Lee, 2000, p. 128; Robson & Pevalin, 2016).[16] Nonetheless, I and others (Liska, 1990) *strongly* disagree. Here's why.

The analysis identifies the model best fitting the data. The statistically significant LR χ^2 test provides an unequivocal answer: mean neighborhood rent deviations across four sides of the board are more than noise.

Group differences more than random noise suggest macro-level, level-2 dynamics are shaping rent values. Those macro-level dynamics merit theoretical consideration (Liska, 1990). "Methodological advances in multilevel modeling are now also leading to theoretical advances in contextual research" (Snijders & Bosker, 2012, p. 12). *Something is going on theoretically at the group level.* Further investigation is warranted.

In sum, dismissing neighborhood rent differences because the intraclass correlation, the level-2 outcome variation, is "trivial," based on some arbitrary cutoff, is scientifically unsound. The results of the statistical test underscore the potential theoretical importance of this variation. Ignoring this level-2 variation closes off potentially important avenues of multilevel theoretical investigation and elaboration (Liska, 1990). Let the LR χ^2 test result for the ANOVA model be the guide, not an arbitrarily chosen value.

Indicators of Model Fit While Controlling for Model Complexity

The post-estimation command `estat ic` produces two indicators of lack-of-model-fit-to-data-while-controlling-for-model-complexity: the Akaike Information Criterion (AIC) (Akaike, 1974) and the Bayesian Information Criterion (BIC) (Raftery, 1995a, 1995b). There are important differences between these two indicators (Vrieze, 2012), so routinely report both. They are similar in

```
168  Akaike's information criterion and Bayesian information criterion
169
170  ----------------------------------------------------------------------
171      Model |        N    ll(null)   ll(model)      df        AIC        BIC
172  ------------+---------------------------------------------------------
173          . |      132        .    -986.1665        3   1978.333   1986.981
174  ----------------------------------------------------------------------
175  Note: BIC uses N = number of observations. See [R] BIC note.
```

Figure 6.4 AIC and BIC values associated with the baseline ANOVA multilevel rent model.

that, with each one, *lower values* reflect a *better* match between model predictions and data, while simultaneously penalizing for higher model complexity.

AIC and BIC values are most useful with generalized multilevel models investigating binary, multinomial, or count outcomes. Nonetheless, if the investigation involves selecting one model over another, *always* generate and save the AIC and BIC values from your ANOVA multilevel model. See Figure 6.4.

The values shown reflect baseline lack of fit. AIC and BIC values from later models with predictors, compared to these baseline values, will reveal which later models more successfully reduced the lack of fit between model predictions and actual data, while simultaneously controlling for variations in complexity across different models. Comparisons apply only when comparing different models of the *same* outcome variable using the *same* dataset. Chapter 8 addresses the question of how much of a change in AIC or BIC indicates noteworthy reductions in lack of fit and provides more background on these two indicators.

Empirical Bayes (EB) Estimation: Explaining Group Mean Adjustments

Bayesian statistics is an entire universe unto itself. The term "Bayesian" comes from Thomas Bayes (1702–1761).[17] There are fully Bayesian statistics (Congdon, 2006; Gelman et al., 2004) and empirical Bayesian statistics. The latter is of concern here.

There is a lot going on "under the hood" when multilevel models generate estimates: iterative maximum likelihood using various estimation protocols (Hox, 2010, p. 41), precision weighting (Snijders & Bosker, 2012, pp. 220–222), and empirical Bayes estimation of group mean residuals and also of level-1 predictor coefficient residuals, if the latter are allowed to vary across level-2 groups (Hox, 2010, p. 29).

The u_{0j} values capturing random effects arising from neighborhood differences on the rent outcome can be viewed in three ways. (1) They are *estimates* about population parameter values, assuming observed data were probability sampled from that population. (2) Alternatively, they are values for "latent [hidden] variables" (Snijders & Bosker, 2012, p. 62).[18] (3) Or they are the results when "data information is combined with population information" (Snijders & Bosker, 2012, p. 62).

In two-level multilevel ANOVA models, EB adjustments generate estimated level-2 means that have been *shrunken toward* or *biased toward* the overall adjusted mean outcome score.[19] The same idea, but for group slopes rather than group means, applies later when allowing each level-2 group its own slope for a predictor. In that case, level-2 β weight deviations are shrunken toward the overall β weight (Chapter 8).

Conceptually, Why Shrink or Adjust Group Means Toward the Estimated Overall Mean?

(1) The analysis seeks to estimate, for each group's mean outcome score, what that group's *true* mean outcome score would be. From each group's mean rent, it derives a population estimate, assuming the records were probability sampled.

(2) As the analysis estimates each level-2 group's true mean score on the outcome, it treats each group mean as part of the larger set of group-level rent averages in the observed data, recognizing that the larger set clusters around an overall mean rent.[20] Thus, when estimating the "true" neighborhood mean rent for properties at different stages of development between Pacific Avenue and the Boardwalk, it examines the other three neighborhood mean rent values.[21] The program simultaneously examines each group mean in the context of the entire dataset including the other group means, their values, their reliabilities, and their positions relative to the overall mean.

How Much to Shrink or Adjust TOWARD the Estimated Overall Mean?

The question then becomes: How much is each level-2 neighborhood's mean rent *shrunken* toward the overall adjusted mean rent? The discrepancy between each shrunken neighborhood mean rent and overall adjusted mean rent creates u_{0j} values. These reflect how much each neighborhood's estimated true mean deviates from the estimated overall mean. The degree of empirical Bayes shrinkage varies by group. Shrinkage is greater; that is, neighborhood average rents are adjusted *more* toward the overall adjusted mean rent, the more each of the following conditions hold for that level-2 neighborhood rent average:

1. It is *farther* from the overall mean.
2. The cases within that group *disagree more* with one another on rent values, thus within-group variation on the outcome score is larger.

3. There are *fewer* cases in the group.
4. All the group means, as a set, are *not* widely dispersed.[22]

To see this graphically, consider Figure 6.5. The darker bars show original rent values for all properties at all stages of development, averaged by neighborhood, for each side of the Monopoly board. The lighter bars show EB-adjusted group mean rent values ($u_{0j} + \gamma_{00}$) for each neighborhood.

Note the following:

(1) Each neighborhood rent average is adjusted some.
(2) All the EB adjustments are *toward* adjusted overall average rent. Those above the overall mean are adjusted downward; those below the overall mean are adjusted upward.
(3) More extreme group means are adjusted more. So group means farther from the overall mean are shrunken more toward the adjusted overall mean rent. More specifically, the gap between lighter and darker bar heights is bigger for records from the first side of the board (sidezero = 0, Mediterranean to Connecticut) where rent is the lowest, and for records from the last side of the board (sidezero = 3, Pacific to Boardwalk), where rent is the

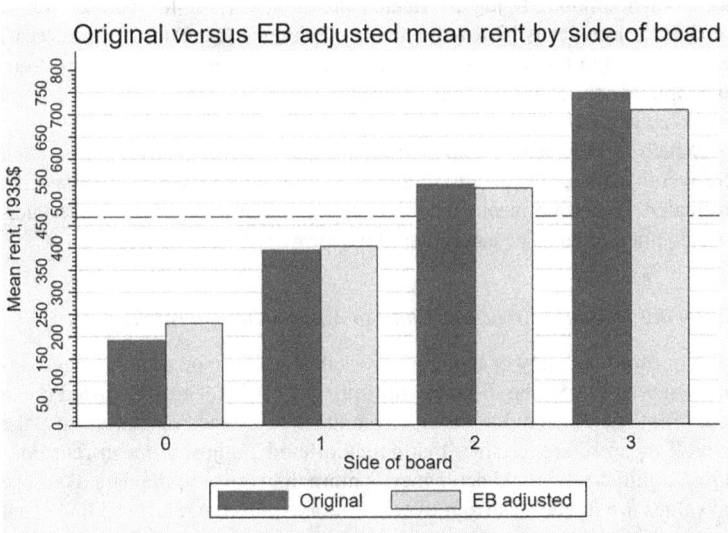

Figure 6.5 Raw rent means by group and empirically Bayes-adjusted rent means by group. The horizontal line ($469.12) references precision-weighted overall average rent (γ_{00}) from the mixed-effects ANOVA model results in Figure 6.2. Side of board = 0 references the first side of the playing board.

highest. This is in contrast to the gaps between original and EB-adjusted means for the two sides of the board in the middle (`sidezero = 1`, St. Charles Place to New York Avenue, or 2, Kentucky Avenue to Marvin Gardens), where the darker/lighter gaps are smaller by comparison. The means for these last two neighborhoods were adjusted less.

Because of this shrinkage adjusting neighborhood rent averages toward the overall adjusted mean, the between-group rent variation, the intraclass correlation is .172 rather than the earlier R^2 value, .188 (Figure 5.6). The .172 value is based on EB-estimated true neighborhood mean rent values. The .188 value is based on observed neighborhood rent averages.

Post-Estimation: Group Pairwise Comparisons

The last chapter considered which neighborhood rent averages were significantly different from one another (Table 5.3). This question can be revisited using EB estimates of these averages. A standard error bar chart in the form of a caterpillar plot provides the evidence. Details on the steps appear in the Chapter 6 `do` file.

In short: adjusted neighborhood mean rent deviations ($u_{0j} - \gamma_{00}$), along with their standard errors, are saved to a file with just four records, one for each neighborhood. Using a selected probability level for comparison, a confidence interval is built around each deviation. The confidence intervals are plotted from the smallest to the largest group mean rent deviation. Non-overlapping confidence intervals indicate significantly different neighborhood rent averages.

Which specific estimated true group means, formatted as residuals around the overall adjusted mean, are significantly different from which other specific estimated true group means? Significantly different means confidence intervals do not overlap. The caterpillar plot appears in Figure 6.6.

Using the Standard Error Bar Chart to Answer Two Questions

First question: are any of the four adjusted neighborhood rent averages significantly ($p < .05$) above or significantly below the overall adjusted mean rent ($\$469.12$)? If a neighborhood's confidence interval *does not* cross the overall mean reference line, that neighborhood's adjusted mean rent *does* differ significantly; the discrepancy is more than noise in the data. Because u_{0j} values are deviations from overall average rent, the reference line is set to zero.

Figure 6.6 shows the following: (1) Rent on the second side of the board (St. Charles Place to New York Avenue) is *not* significantly *cheaper* than average overall rent; the confidence interval includes the reference

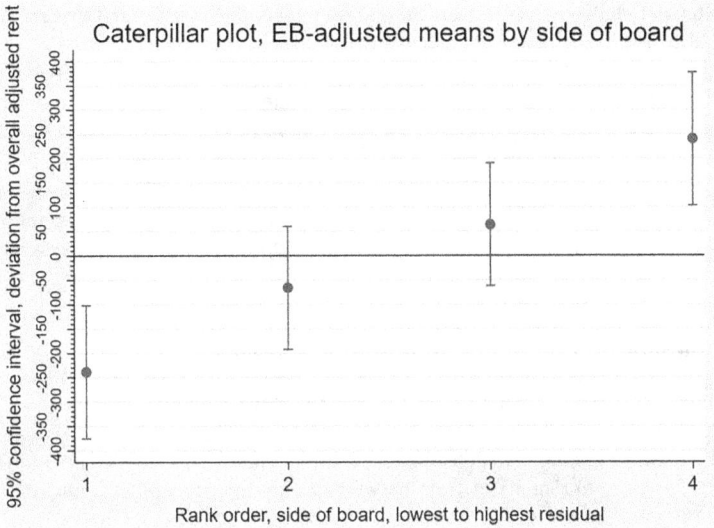

Figure 6.6 Standard error bar chart/caterpillar plot with 95% confidence intervals. EB-adjusted side-of-board means are expressed as residuals around the overall mean adjusted rent; u_0 values are from the ANOVA mixed-effects model (Figure 6.2). The horizontal reference line at 0 corresponds to the adjusted overall mean rent, γ_{00}, \$469.12.

line. (2) Rent on the third side of the board (Kentucky Avenue to Marvin Gardens) is *not* significantly *more expensive* than average overall rent. Again, the confidence interval includes the overall adjusted mean. (3) Rent for one group of properties, from Mediterranean to Connecticut, *is* significantly cheaper than average. The confidence interval for this neighborhood average does *not* include the overall adjusted average.[23] (4) Average rent for properties from Pacific Avenue to Boardwalk significantly exceeds the overall average. The confidence interval does not include the reference line.

Second question: are adjusted neighborhood rent averages on *any one side* of the board significantly ($p < .05$) different from those on *any other side?* In the caterpillar plot, any *pair* of *non-overlapping* confidence intervals indicates two neighborhood rent averages whose difference is more than random noise.

Examine Figure 6.6. Note the following: (1) Rent on the first side of the board (Mediterranean to Connecticut) is significantly cheaper than rent on the third side of the board (Kentucky to Marvin Gardens). (2) Rent on the first side of the board is significantly cheaper than rent on the fourth side of the board (Pacific to Boardwalk). (3) Rent on the second side of the board

(St. Charles Place to New York Ave.) is significantly cheaper than rent on the fourth side of the board (Pacific to Boardwalk).

Do pairwise comparisons align with ANOVA post hoc Scheffé test results? They do. Table 5.3 shows the exact same pattern of statistically significant pairwise differences (using the `sidezero` variable: 0 < 2, 0 < 3, 1 < 3; using the `side` variable: 1 < 3, 1 < 4, 2 < 4). Therefore, even after empirical Bayes adjustments, the pairwise pattern of statistically significant versus non-statistically-significant pairwise group rent discrepancies remains the same. This just *happens* to be true here. With different data, there may not be agreement between these two approaches.

Summary of the ANOVA Submodel

Some key takeaway points about the ANOVA multilevel model.

(1) It generates a more robust estimate, a population estimate, of how much variation in rent arises from between-group differences, here, four varying neighborhood rent averages. The between-group outcome variation, expressed as a proportion of total outcome variation, is the intraclass correlation (ρ or r_{icc}).

(2) Even if the intraclass correlation seems descriptively small, do not dismiss it if it is statistically significant. A significant likelihood ratio χ^2 test in the ANOVA model signifies the need for a multilevel model with random intercepts for the different level-2 groups.

(3) Remember, this is about theory as well as stats. A significant likelihood ratio χ^2 test in the ANOVA model means level-2 theoretical processes are influencing outcome values. This may well be consequential for relevant theory (Liska, 1990). It raises additional questions. What are these dynamics? Can level-2 indicators be developed to reflect relevant level-2 theoretical constructs?

(4) The ANOVA model with no predictors generates baseline estimates of the lack of fit between the data predicted by model features and the observed data, while controlling for model complexity. Bayes Information Criterion (BIC) and Akaike Information Criterion (AIC) values should be generated with the ANOVA model and retained. Lower values indicate better model-data match. Save BIC and AIC baseline values.[24]

(5) Empirical Bayes adjustments shrink observed level-2 outcome means toward the overall adjusted outcome mean. EB-adjusted group means, u_{0j} values, are latent variables approximating population estimates of each group's average outcome score. They are expressed as deviations from the overall adjusted mean (γ_{00}).

(6) Multilevel models adjust the overall mean outcome (γ_{00}) using precision weighting.

Notes

1 This is Raudenbush and Bryk's (2002, p. 23) Eq. 2.7. Additional assumptions, not detailed here, apply to this model.
2 Some texts will use μ [lower case Greek letter "mu"] rather than γ for the "population grand mean" (Snijders & Bosker, 2012, pp. 17–18, Eq. 3.1). Snijders and Bosker's equation is a combined model. The equation shown here is just for Level 2.
3 Either capital U (Snijders & Bosker, 2012, p. 29) or lowercase u can be used.
4 Precision weighting takes into account varying numbers of records across the level-2 groups. Further, group means that are more precise are those where the within-group variance on the outcome variable is less, i.e., different records within a group are more similar on the variable in question. Groups with more precise group means contribute more to the overall, precision-weighted average (Raudenbush & Bryk, 2002, p. 40).
5 I know of no hard-and-fast rule about the minimum number of level-2 units needed if level-2 units are sampled from a larger population of level-2 units. The numbers proposed here are just a *rough* guideline. A precise answer considers several factors, including estimated level-2 statistical power levels. Multilevel power estimation programs are available (Browne et al., 2023; Spybrook et al., 2011).
6 Some books show the variance as τ_{00} (Raudenbush & Bryk, 2002, p. 47), while others show it as τ^2_0 (Snijders & Bosker, 2012, p. 75, Eq. 5.4). The different terms reference the same parameter.
7 Here, and in other figures showing Stata output, line numbers are from a Notepad++ printout of the Stata `log` file. Your specific line numbers may differ if you add/subtract lines from the `do` file.
8 Sometimes the iterations can go on and on . . . and on and on and on. It can become an issue especially with generalized models dealing with outcomes like binary variables or counts (Hox, 2010, p. 119). Getting into why that happens goes beyond the current volume's scope.
9 The entire discussion of fixed-effects models, random-effects models, and fixed-effects *portions* of random-effects models can get confusing (Gelman & Hill, 2007, pp. 245–246). The entire model is a random-effects model because it is allowing each group to have a randomly varying mean score on the outcome; this "refers to the randomness in the probability model for the group level coefficients" (Gelman & Hill, 2007, p. 245). Here, the coefficients in question are the values for the group means. Gelman and Hill (2007, p. 246) recommend using terms like varying intercepts, constant slopes, and varying slopes, to describe the model itself. Nonetheless, because terms like fixed-effects models, random-effects models, and fixed and random *portions* of multilevel models are widely used in this literature, I use them here.
10 We have seen *a number very close to* this number before: $469.06, the overall average. There is a reason for this discrepancy. It is not a mistake. It is part of the adjustments the mixed-effects models are making. Skip the rest of this footnote if you do not care about the reason for the discrepancy.
  In some cases, γ_{00} is *not necessarily the overall average on the outcome score seen in the constant in a monolevel regression*. This is because, in a multilevel model, γ_{00} is a "*precision weighted average*" also "commonly called the *weighted least squares estimator*"; it is the "*maximum likelihood estimator*" (Raudenbush & Bryk, 2002, p. 40) of the overall mean. It might be the same as the average of the group averages if all the groups have the same number of records. But it might diverge if the groups are of different sizes as they are here. Some sides of the board have 30 rents, others have 36. Groups with more records contribute more to the estimated overall average. Further, precision weighting also allows groups to contribute more

to the overall average if they have smaller variances, that is, they are groups whose individual observations have more tightly clustered outcome scores.

11 What you actually see is "$p > |z|$" and ".000". *Never* report "$p < .000$" or "$p = .000$" in any tables. *This would mean that the probability of this result is zero.* All that is happening here is the program is rounding to three decimal places. So $p < .0005$ shows up as .000.

12 For more details see Rabe-Hesketh and Skrondal (2012a, pp. 88–89).

13 Of course, we are not surprised. We already know game designers made properties more expensive as one progresses around the board. It is unlikely when working with real datasets, however, that we will know how the data are structured beforehand.

14 LR tests on later models that include level-1 or level-2 predictors address different questions.

15 There are numerous types of intraclass correlations, and they are widely used to estimate inter-rater reliability (Shrout & Fleiss, 1979, p. 423). The type of intraclass correlation used here is what Shrout and Fleiss (1979) call "ICC(1,1)" and it "takes the form of a variance ratio." It is a population estimate.

16 Robson and Pevalin (2016) cite Lee (2000) on this point. Lee (2000, p. 128), discussing school context effects, suggests that "only when the ICC is more than trivial (i.e., greater than 10% of the total variance in the outcome) would the analyst need to consider multilevel methods." In other words, Lee is suggesting you *can* ignore the clustered data structure, proceed with a monolevel model, and ignore the between-group mean differences, if the ICC is less than 10%, because such an amount is "trivial."

17 He "was a reputable mathematician and Presbyterian minister in England" who invented Bayes' Theorem, also known as Bayes' Rule (Kruschke, 2011, p. 62). Bayesian inference "gets us from prior to posterior beliefs" where prior beliefs apply before examining the data at hand, and posterior beliefs apply after examining those data (Kruschke, 2011, p. 12). How do views about something change after acquiring additional relevant data? For example, we might believe a single die will end a roll with a "one" facing up about 16–17 percent or 1/6 of the time. This would be our prior belief. But if we roll it 100 times and it comes up "one" 50% of the time, our posterior belief about this die, and its fairness, would be different. Bayes and Laplace in France "receive independent credit as the first to *invert* the probability statement and obtain probability statements about θ [Greek small letter theta], *given* observed *y*" (Gelman et al., 2004, p. 34). θ "denote[s] unobservable vector quantities or population parameters of interest" (Gelman et al., 2004, p. 5). Instead of saying "how likely are these data?" a Bayesian asks: "*given* these data, how likely is my model feature?"

18 "They are so-called Empirical Bayes (EB) or *shrinkage* estimates: a weighted average of the specific OLS estimates in each class [here, group] and the overall regression coefficient, estimated for all similar classes [here, groups]" (Hox, 2010, p. 29).

19 "Because of this shrinkage effect, empirical Bayes estimates are biased [toward the overall intercept, or overall *b* weight]. However, they are usually more precise, a property that is often more useful than being unbiased" (Hox, 2010, p. 30). For more technical detail, see (Hox, 2010, p. 30, Eq. 2.14). Further, "the shrinkage estimator . . . protects us against capitalizing on chance" (Raudenbush & Bryk, 2002, p. 157).

20 The term "overall mean" is used loosely here. The analysis here is considering a "precision weighted average" as the appropriate value for the overall mean, γ_{00}, not the arithmetic mean (Raudenbush & Bryk, 2002, p. 40). Precision weighting takes into account that "the residual standard deviations of some cases [group means here] are larger than for others, and estimates will be more precise if cases with higher residual standard deviation get lower weight" (Snijders & Bosker, 2012, p. 220).

21 Of course, the Monopoly dataset is using the population of rent values to derive mean rent values for each side of the board, not sample data. *But the analysis does not know this.* So it is going to assume these are means based on probability-sampled values.

22 "If the group sizes are small *and there is little variation across groups*, the reliability λ_j [of the group means] is close to 0.0, and more weight is put on the overall estimate γ_{00}" in estimating true group means (Hox et al., 2018, p. 244 emphasis added).

23 This last point partially aligns with one statistician's findings about return on investment when playing the Monopoly game: "By far the worst individual investment is to buy Mediterranean Avenue without first owning Baltic. That's not to say that you shouldn't buy it, but it's not going to make you much money without quite a bit of construction" (Collins, 2005). The findings here suggest a slight modification to this game advice. On average, *all* of the properties on this side of the board are going to be *significantly* less revenue-producing than an average property.

24 Strictly speaking, AIC and BIC are not needed for models with normally distributed outcomes. But they are essential for model selection. When working with non-normal outcomes like binary, count, or multinomial outcomes, you will need them. Suggest getting used to working with them sooner rather than later.

7 Second Multilevel Model

Adding Guesthouses and Hotels

All Guesthouses and Hotels Not Created Equal

Time to add houses and hotels to models predicting rent.

First, some background on the Monopoly's real estate development rules for readers who have not played. The more developed the property, the higher its rent. Development begins only when all properties of one color are in the hands of one owner. Further, development follows the same pattern for all properties, with guesthouses added evenly across all properties of the same color until there are four on each property of the same color, at which point one hotel on each property can replace the four guesthouses there.

Socioeconomic realities of early 20th century Atlantic City were reflected in these development rules in three ways. (1) Guesthouse and hotel development costs, starting at $50 for properties on the first side of the board, increase by $50 with each turn to the next side of the board. Neighborhood differences in development costs reflected neighborhood variations in land prices and resulted in structures and accommodations of varying quality. (2) Higher quality accommodations in turn charged higher rent. As seen in Chapter 5, rents differ significantly by neighborhood. (3) A more developed property implies more localized demand for its guesthouses or hotel. Thus, the more developed the property, the higher the rent requested.

Underscoring that second point, do not be misled by the identical plastic green guesthouses and red hotels supplied with the game. In early to mid-20th Century Atlantic City, some guesthouses offered a private bath, a sitting room, more furnishings, and dining amenities, while others offered little more than a room with a dresser and a bed, and a shared bath down the hall (Johnson, 2009, p. 158). Hotel quality varied too.

To better visualize variations in accommodation quality, Figure 7.1 shows postcard images of two different guesthouses in different parts of town. Figure 7.2 shows images of two different hotels again in different parts of town.

DOI: 10.4324/9781003392682-7

Figure 7.1 The top panel (A) shows a more modest accommodation, the Abbey Guest-house, 135 Westminster Ave., Atlantic City, NJ.

Source: Boston Public Library, Tichnor Brothers Postcard Collection.

Permalink: https://ark.digitalcommonwealth.org/ark:/50959/4m90dv66n.

The bottom panel (B) shows a somewhat more luxurious accommodation, Tubis Guesthouse, 2903 Pacific Ave., Atlantic City, NJ. Note the sign advertising private baths.

Source: Boston Public Library, Tichnor Brothers Postcard Collection.

Permalink: https://ark.digitalcommonwealth.org/ark:/50959/zk51vh626

Figure 7.2 The top panel (A) shows a more modest hotel, Beacon Hotel, 146 So. Tennessee Avenue, Atlantic City, NJ.

Source: Boston Public Library, Tichnor Brothers Postcard Collection.

Permalink: https://ark.digitalcommonwealth.org/ark:/50959/x920gc54r.

The bottom panel (B) shows a fancier accommodation, Hotel Marlborough House at Boardwalk and Park Place, Atlantic City, NJ.

Source: Library of Congress, Prints and Photographs Online Catalog. www.loc.gov/pictures/item/2016794704/

A Thought Experiment and Two Types of Questions

Hedonic regressions of house prices show that variations in house prices are driven not only by location differentials, like access to higher quality schools and parks, but also by the amenities of the house itself: square footage, number of bedrooms, number of bathrooms, lot size, and so on (Dubin & Goodman, 1982; Troy & Grove, 2008). Even after taking house and lot features into account, buyers are willing to pay more for houses in higher SES neighborhoods (Dubin & Sung, 1990).

Apply these hedonic house price ideas to Monopoly renters. Consider three factors affecting how much renters pay to stay at Monopoly properties at different stages of development.

(1) A more developed property – more guesthouses, or a hotel – implies more demand for rentals at that location, and higher demand means higher rent prices. This would be a within-neighborhood or level-1 effect.

(2) A property in a higher SES neighborhood with better access to entertainment venues and the ocean-side beach can charge higher rents. This would be a between-neighborhood or level-2 effect.

(3) Now, the first piece of the thought experiment. Imagine a third factor: the Monopoly game includes renter ratings of accommodation satisfaction, like a current-day TripAdvisor® rating, for each property at each stage of development. Rent impacts of accommodation quality ratings could vary at level 1, capturing establishment differences within neighborhoods. Two guesthouses in the same neighborhood might offer varying qualities of service, leading to different levels of guest satisfaction. Alternatively, accommodation quality ratings could differ at level 2, reflecting between-neighborhood differences in atmosphere. Finally, these ratings could reflect both level-1 and level-2 variations in guest satisfaction.

Neighborhood Effects Questions

Now, the second piece of the thought experiment. After controlling for two of the above-mentioned factors – (1), level of property development, and (3), hypothetical accommodation quality ratings – are the significant level-2, between-neighborhood rent impacts observed in Chapter 6 (Figure 6.2) affected? Do the between-neighborhood rent differences shrink? If so, by how much? Are the remaining between-neighborhood differences still more than random noise?

Call these *neighborhood effects* questions.[1] With these questions, the focus is on neighborhood effects while controlling for differences in the composition of housing accommodations. Compositional differences include above factors (1) and (3), recognizing that differences in the latter, the hypothetical TripAdvisor® quality ratings, could have a between-neighborhood as well as a within-neighborhood component.

Compositional Effects Questions

Now, the third and final piece of the thought experiment. Suppose interest centered on a different type of question. It is a given that accommodation quality varies across neighborhoods. This is reflected in higher costs for purchasing guesthouses and hotels in higher SES neighborhoods. It is also reflected in higher average rents in higher SES neighborhoods (Figure 6.6) and variations in the hypothetical TripAdvisor® accommodation ratings. Here is the question: does the within-neighborhood composition of real estate affect rent, after controlling for between-neighborhood rent differences? More specifically, once between-neighborhood differences are completely removed, is there a significant rent impact of the number of guesthouses? How about the rent impact of a hotel being present?

Call these *compositional effects* questions. These questions seek to isolate within-neighborhood rent impacts of levels of real estate development on a property, while completely controlling for between-neighborhood rent differences.[2]

These Are Analysis of Covariance (ANCOVA) Questions

Although the dataset lacks accommodation quality ratings, the neighborhood effects and compositional effects questions each can be addressed using one type of analysis: multilevel analysis of covariance or multilevel ANCOVA. n_house and hotel are the level-1 explanatory variables. Each level-1 predictor can have one average impact on rent. Rent observations at level 1 ($n = 132$) are grouped by neighborhood at level 2 ($n = 4$).

> If there are no higher-level explanatory variables, this model is equivalent to a random effects analysis of covariance (ANCOVA); the grouping variable is the usual ANCOVA factor, and the lowest-level [level-1] explanatory variables are the covariates . . . ANCOVA uses OLS techniques and multilevel regression uses ML estimation. Nevertheless, both models are highly similar.
>
> (Hox, 2010, p. 57)

Time for just one equation to summarize.

The ANCOVA combined rent model can be written as (after Hox, 2010, p. 56, Eq. 4.4):

$$Y_{ij} = \gamma_{00} + \gamma_{10}X_{1ij} + \gamma_{20}X_{2ij} + u_{0j} + r_{ij} \tag{Eq. 7.1}$$

Where

1. $Y_{ij} =$ individual rent observation
2. $\gamma_{00} =$ overall average adjusted rent when both level-1 predictors score 0

3. γ_{10} = average rent impact of n_house
4. X_{1ij} = level-1 values for n_house
5. γ_{20} = average rent impact of hotel
6. X_{2ij} = level-1 values for hotel
7. u_{0j} = level-2 neighborhood-level rent residuals after controlling for development
8. r_{ij} = level-1 within-neighborhood rent residuals after controlling for development

Before launching the ANCOVA model, however, a short but important side trip is needed to clear up a misunderstanding. Sometimes scholarly work appearing in good refereed journals misunderstands which multilevel models do and which do not completely remove level-2 outcome differences.

How to Completely Remove Level-2 Neighborhood Outcome Differences

ANCOVA Model Portions

The ANCOVA has a *fixed-effects-model portion*. That is the part of your results describing impacts of specific level-1 predictors or, if included, specific level-2 predictors. These include parameters in lines 3 and 5.

It also has a *random-effects-model portion*. This includes u_{0j} values in line 7 and their variance, τ_{00}.

This ANCOVA Model Does Not Control for Neighborhood Differences Because of What it Assumes

This model, however, does not control for neighborhood (side-of-board) differences when describing the impacts of and significance of level-1 predictors. Allowing each neighborhood's residualized average rent to vary randomly might not completely remove neighborhood rent differences. This is because the model makes an important – and perhaps flawed – assumption.

The model assumes no significant correlation between residual neighborhood mean rent deviations and scores on level-1 predictors. See Figure 7.3. The dotted line connecting the level-2 residual neighborhood differences and the level-1 predictors n_house and hotel reflects assumed negligible correlations between level-1 predictor scores and residual neighborhood rent differences.

Flawed Assumption?

This assumption could be wrong.[3] There might be noteworthy correlations between these residual neighborhood mean rent differences and level-1 predictor scores.

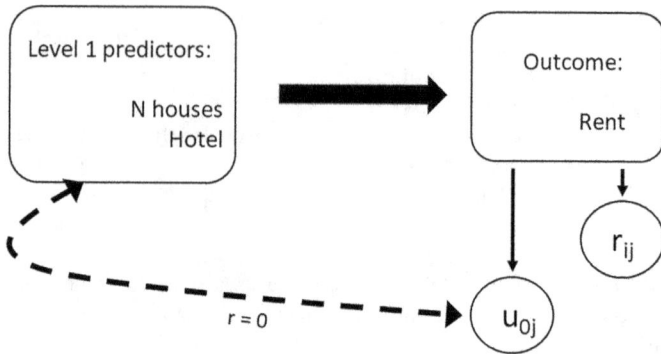

Note. Multilevel model with **random effects** at level 2. r_{ij} = level 1 residuals; u_{0j} = level-2 residuals. Dashed double headed arrow indicates that scores on predictors are **assumed** to correlate zero (r = 0) with level-2 residuals. This assumption may not be correct.

Figure 7.3 Multilevel ANCOVA rent model with random effects at neighborhood level.

Since the ANCOVA model has at least one predictor, remaining neighborhood rent variations, u_{0j} values, are residuals. A sizable correlation between level-1 predictor scores and level-2 residuals would be problematic. Residual neighborhood differences could be affecting outcome scores via their link to predictor scores.

This is a multilevel counterpart to a well-known OLS regression problem. OLS "assumptions . . . ensure independence of errors and X variables, which is sufficient for unbiased estimation of all β_k parameters" (Hamilton, 1992, p. 110). Violating this assumption can lead to "invalid t and F tests" (Hamilton, 1992, p. 113, Table 4.1).

In the multilevel context, there are residuals at two levels (elements 7 and 8). Additional assumptions about residuals apply in the multilevel model context (Hox, 2010, pp. 23–28). Assumptions about level-2 residuals are particularly crucial.[4] If level-2 residuals violate assumptions, and link to predictor scores, estimates of level-1 predictor rent impacts could be tainted. A level-1 estimated predictor impact could reflect the combined impact of *both* (1) the level-1 predictor and (2) the associated, unmeasured portion of residual neighborhood differences tied in with predictor scores. In simpler terms, the influences of remaining neighborhood differences (u_{0j} values) has not been completely separated from impacts of level-1 predictors.

How to Check

There are two approaches. The first conducts model residual diagnostics, including examining plots linking predictor scores and residual neighborhood differences, for each predictor (Snijders & Bosker, 2012, pp. 161–167). The checking protocol becomes onerous with numerous predictors.

Alternatively, *completely remove all between-neighborhood differences*, including unobserved differences. Doing so requires a different model setup: a fixed-effects model of neighborhood effects. This is similar to the regression operation in Chapter 5 using `i.sidezero` that turned `sidezero` into a factor variable.

Enter a dummy (0/1) or indicator variable for each of the last three sides of the board. Dummy variables are "black boxes." Each one accounts for *all* rent differences between that side of the board and the first side of the board. Such a model takes care of correlations – any correlations! – between level-1 predictors and neighborhood differences. Table 7.1 shows how the four neighborhoods could be coded on three dummy variables.[5] In datasets with large numbers of level-2 units, it can be more convenient to allow the program to enter this large number of dummy variables "behind the scenes." This is now a fixed effects model.

Fixed Effects Model Assumptions and Consequences

Model assumptions have shifted. See Figure 7.4. The fixed-effects model for neighborhood effects assumes that residual between-neighborhood rent differences *might* correlate with scores on level-1 predictors. It takes care of that because the three neighborhood dummy variables completely remove *all* between-neighborhood rent differences. Only within-neighborhood rent variation, pooled across all four neighborhoods, remains.

Consequently, *b* weights for `n_house` and `hotel` are *completely decontaminated* from neighborhood effects. Now – and only now! – does the multilevel model reveal impacts of development after *completely controlling for* neighborhood differences.

Table 7.1 Coding of three dummy variables for fixed effects model of neighborhood effects

Side of board where properties located	Dummy coded variables: Names and values		
	side2_01	side3_01	side4_01
Pass Go➜Jail	0	0	0
Jail➜Free parking	1	0	0
Free Parking ➜Go directly to jail	0	1	0
Go directly to jail➜Pass Go	0	0	1

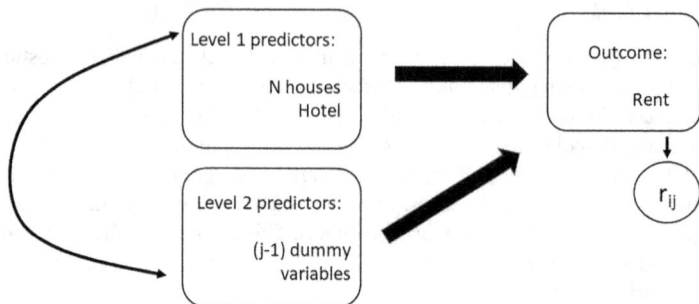

Note. Multilevel model with **fixed effects** at level 2. r_{ij} = level 1 residuals. There is no level-2 residual because the (j-1) dummy variables remove all level-2 outcome variation. Model assumes that the level-1 predictors and the level-2 predictors might correlate with one another.

Figure 7.4 ANCOVA rent model with fixed effects at neighborhood level.

If the researcher's primary focus is estimating compositional effects after completely removing neighborhood effects, this is the preferred approach. Note, however, three additional points about the fixed effects model.

(1) It changes the *meaning* of the level-1 b weights. Each now only captures level-1 or within-neighborhood impacts. For example, the *b* weight for `hotel` would now only reflect rent impacts when contrasting rents *within the same neighborhood*. This may or may not be the answer sought.
(2) The neighborhood fixed effects model will not be the best answer if there is theoretical interest in impacts of *specific* neighborhood-level predictors (see Chapter 10). After entering the (j-1) level-2 indicator variables, no additional level-2 predictors are possible.
(3) With a large number of level-2 units, and some data file structures, fixed effects at level-2 might create an incidental parameters problem (Lancaster, 2001).

Monopoly Example Details

Time for some results. This model examines rent impacts of the level of real estate development – n_house and `hotel` – taking account of neighborhood differences. These level-2 differences are modeled in four different ways. Table 7.2 shows the results.[6]

Table 7.2 Four ANCOVA models predicting rent in 1935$ and controlling for level of development

		Model_1	Model_2	Model_3	Model_4
Predictors					
1	N houses	$215.786	$215.786	$215.786	$215.786
2		($18.039)	($49.402)	($12.332)	($12.236)
3		11.962	4.368	17.498	17.636
4		< .001	< .05	< .001	< .001
5	Hotel present (1) or not (0)	$1,060.518	$1,060.518	$1,060.518	$1,060.518
6		($72.156)	($203.352)	($49.328)	($48.942)
7		14.697	5.215	21.499	21.669
8		< .001	< .05	< .001	< .001
9	Side of board				
10	2			$202.411	
11				($45.217)	
12				4.476	
13				< .001	
14	3			$349.856	
15				($45.217)	
16				7.737	
17				< .001	
18	4			$555.467	
19				($47.228)	
20				11.761	
21				< .001	
22	Intercept	−$67.336	−$67.336	−$344.197	−$67.265
Random effects (RE) portion					
23	var(_cons)				$40,120.580
24					($29,137.704)
25	var(e)				$32,936.236
26					($4,117.279)
Model details					
27	N observations	132	132	132	132
28	R-squared	0.655	0.655	0.842	
29	F statistic	122.197	185.828	134.595	
30	Log likelihood	−923.58	−923.58	−871.82	−881.28
31	χ^2				531.21
32	Model test $p <$				< .001
33	N RE parameters				2.00
34	N variances				2.00
35	Neighborhood FE?	No	No	Yes	No
36	Robust se?	No	Yes	No	Indirectly

(*Continued*)

Table 7.2 (Continued)

		Model_1	Model_2	Model_3	Model_4
Predictors					
37	N groups analyzed	1	1	1	4
38	Neighborhood RE	No	No	No	Yes

Note: Model 1 = OLS regression. Model 2 = same but with robust standard errors. Model 3 = OLS regression with fixed effects for neighborhood (side of playing board) differences. Model 4 = multilevel model with random level-2 effects. Standard errors in parentheses. Fixed effects portion shows b/se/t / p <. var(_cons) = level-2 residual variance. Level 2 = different sides of the board. var(e) = level-1 residual variance. Level 1 = individual rent observation. χ^2 for model tests null hypothesis that the variation in the outcome explained by the predictors is only random noise. A different and significant χ^2 positioned below the table of results in the log file and labeled "LR test vs. linear model" confirms that important, not-yet-explained level 2 differences across the four groups remain.

Reviewing Results Line by Line

Four different models appear

1. Model 1 corresponds to a standard OLS multiple regression. Neighborhood differences are ignored.
2. Model 2 is an OLS multiple regression with robust standard errors specified. It recognizes correlated errors within level-2 groups and appropriately widens standard errors. In effect, the model acknowledges violating the assumption of independent error terms. This approach has advocates (White, 1982) and detractors (Freedman, 2006).
3. Model 3 is a fixed-effects OLS model. As in Chapter 5, three neighborhood dummy variables enter. i.side is used rather than i.sidezero, so the dummy variable names align with the named side of the board.[7] These three dummy variables capture all of the level-2, between-neighborhood rent variation.
4. Model 4 is a random effects ANCOVA model, allowing each neighborhood's average rent residual to vary randomly. Each side of the board has its own deviation from predicted rent after controlling for the predictors entered. This model, as discussed previously, does *not* completely control for between-neighborhood rent differences when estimating level-1 predictors' rent impacts.

Lines 1 through 4 in Table 7.2 show the predicted impact of an additional guesthouse on rent. What is being controlled for depends on the specific model. Nevertheless, each additional guesthouse is predicted to elevate rent

$215.79. This is the cost of vacationing on a more developed street with more guesthouses.

The guesthouse *b* weight is identical in each model. This is *just* a reflection of game design. With other data, the estimated impact of a level-1 predictor could shift across models.

Immediately below the *b* weight is its standard error. It varies dramatically across models, being smallest with the mixed-effects model (4), and largest with the OLS clustered errors model (2). The standard errors under this latter option are about 2.5 to 4 times larger than the standard errors in the other models.

Given varying standard errors, of course *t* statistics vary as well. *t* values are smallest ($p = .02$) under the clustered errors model and largest in the mixed-effects model ($p < .001$).

Lines 5–8 reference predicted hotel impacts. Again, the *b* weight is identical across models ($1,060.52), but standard errors, *t* values, and significance levels vary.

Lines 10 through 21 apply only to Model 3, the OLS model with fixed-effects at the neighborhood level. Three dummy variables for the last three sides of the board capture *all* between-neighborhood rent differences. Each associated *b* weight contrasts the predicted average rent difference between that side of the board and the first side of the board, from Mediterranean to Connecticut Avenues, for properties at an average stage of development, which is between two and the guesthouses. In each case, the contrast is more than random noise in the data.

Some subtraction reveals the predicted rent jumps when turning each corner of the playing board, for an average development stage. Going from the first side of the board to the second side of the board (St. Charles Place to New York Ave.) elevates predicted rent $202.41. Making the turn past Free Parking to the third side of the board predicted rent jumps less dramatically ($349.86 − $202.41 = $147.45). Making the last turn past the police officer, from the third to the fourth side of the board, predicted rent jumps a bit more ($555.47 − $349.86 = $205.61).

Line 22 describes the constant or intercept. It is not interpretable given its negative value.

Model 3, the fixed effect model, completely removes *all* neighborhood level rent variation with its three level-2 dummy variables. Zero neighborhood-level rent differences remain.

In Model 3, Lines 1–8 show fixed effect impacts, or average impacts, of level-1 predictors in this fixed effects model. *Although the b weights are identical to those shown in the other models because of the dataset structure, the interpretation is different.* The *b* weights capture *only* predicted within-neighborhood rent impacts of development. More broadly,

74   *Second Multilevel Model*

these capture development compositional effects net of neighborhood differences.

Turning to Model 4, the multilevel, random effects model, lines 1–8 represent the fixed-effects *portion* of the model: predicted average rent impacts of n_house and hotel. Lines 23–26 present the random-effects *portion* of the multilevel model: residual level-1 and level-2 rent variation after controlling for development levels. Only Model 4 provides these estimates because it is the only one separating rent into level-1 and level-2 outcome variation buckets. This model explicitly anticipates neighborhood-level random effects; see line 37.

Level-1 and level-2 variances appeared in the ANOVA model (Figure 6.2). Now, however, these variances reflect neighborhood *residual* rent differences ($40,120.58) and observation-within-neighborhood *residual* differences ($32,936.24). This is how much unexplained rent variation remains after controlling for development levels.

Each residual variance estimate has an associated standard error. The latter reflects the uncertainty associated with sampling error, assuming the data records were sampled from a population.

Explained Variance (R^2) in Single-Level Models

Examine line 28, showing the typical OLS R^2 values.

Explained variation, as a percentage of all the outcome variation, is the same for Models 1 and 2: 65.5%. Model 2, as noted earlier, just modified the standard errors by allowing clustered rather than independent error terms. In Model 3, however, the R^2 value is much higher: 84.2% rather than 65.5%. Whence the additional 18.78% explained variation? The answer is these are the neighborhood effects on rent, captured by the three neighborhood dummies in Model 3.[8]

Explained Variance (R^2) in Multilevel Models

Model 4 shows no entry for R^2. What happened? You can get an R^2 value for Model 4; in fact, you can get three R^2 values. You could obtain

1. A level-1 R^2 describing how much level-1, within-neighborhood rent variation was explained;
2. A level-2 R^2 describing how much level-2 rent variation was explained; and
3. A total R^2.

Before deciding which one to choose, and getting into calculations, consider what is happening conceptually.

Proportional Reduction in Error (PRE)

In monolevel multiple regression, you can think about R^2 in several different ways. One way is "as the proportional reduction in the unexplained [*Y*] variance, due to the use of the [predictor] variables," which is the same as "the proportional reduction in the mean square error of prediction" (Snijders & Bosker, 1994, p. 101). More simply:

$$R^2 = 1 - \left[\frac{(variance\ of\ residuals)\,/}{(variance\ of\ original\ observed\ outcome\ scores)} \right] \quad \text{(Eq. 7.2)}$$

"The same principle can be used to define 'explained proportion of variance' in the hierarchical linear model" (Snijders & Bosker, 1994, p. 101).

PRE and the Buckets

Review Figure 6.3, which separated unexplained outcome variance into its level-1 and level-2 buckets. Now consider adding a third bucket that holds *all* the water – all the unexplained rent variance ($204,954.46) – from both buckets. See Figure 7.5. This is the situation in the ANOVA model, before predictors enter. Predictors have not yet removed – explained away – any of the rent variation in any bucket because there are no predictors.

The multilevel ANCOVA model (Model 4, Table 7.2) entered predictors which took water – unexplained variation – out of each bucket. This lowered

Figure 7.5   Three buckets for unexplained variation in the ANCOVA multilevel model. All the buckets are full because no predictors have been entered yet.

the level of water *remaining*, the residual unexplained rent variation, in each bucket. For R^2 values, applying the PRE framework:

$$\text{PRE} = 1 - \left(\frac{\text{water volume in } \textit{each} \text{ bucket } \textit{after} \text{ entering predictors}}{\text{initial water volume in the bucket}} \right)$$

(Eq. 7.3)

In short, one can

treat proportional reductions in the estimated variance components, σ^2 [level-1] and τ_0^2 [level-2] in the random-intercept model for two levels, as analogs of R^2-values. Since there are several variance components in the hierarchical linear model, this approach leads to several R^2 values, one for each component.

(Snijders & Bosker, 2012, p. 109)

In a two-level model like the one here, "the proportional reduction of error for predicting an individual outcome" is "the first, and most important" (Snijders & Bosker, 2012, p. 111) reduction in error to understand. Therefore, level-1 PRE would be most important. But there is also level-2 explained variance, "the proportional reduction of error for predicting a group mean," which might be "of less practical importance" depending on the situation (Snijders & Bosker, 2012, p. 111).

Less attention is given here to level-2 R^2 given several complexities: (1) Calculating that value requires taking different group sizes into account, making matters more complex (Snijders & Bosker, 1994, pp. 103–106). (2) Tangling matters more, there are different ways to think about different group sizes although those different approaches may provide comparable results (Hox, 2010, p. 77). (3) Research articles by well-respected scholars sometimes report level-2 R^2 values without previously describing the intraclass correlation. A level-2 R^2 of 90% sounds impressive; 90% of 10% sounds less impressive. (4) A final drawback is that under some conditions, a level-2 R^2 value is "a negative R^2 . . . [which] is an impossible value" (Hox, 2010, p. 72).

More specifically, the focus on proportional reduction of outcome variance in *each* "bucket" is a

definition of R^2 [which] now and then leads to unpleasant surprises: it sometimes happens that adding explanatory variables *increases* rather than decreases some of the variance components. Even negative values of R^2 are possible. Negative values of R^2 are clearly undesirable and are not in accordance with its intuitive interpretation.

(Snijders & Bosker, 2012, p. 109)

In other words, a model with predictors might *raise* rather than *lower* the water level reflecting residual unexplained variance in the level-2 bucket. This is what a negative R^2 means (Snijders & Bosker, 2012, p. 110, Table 7.1). With predictors added, unexplained outcome variation in the level-2 bucket can rise above its initial level, overflowing the bucket.

Comparing ANOVA variance numbers (Figure 6.3) with no predictors, to the variance numbers in the ANCOVA multilevel model here (Model 4, Table 7.2), shows this is what has happened here. Unexplained level-2 *residual* rent variance ($40,121) was more than level-2 *initial* unexplained variance ($35,277). The level-2 bucket started to overflow.

Why? A full explanation gets beyond the focus on fundamentals in this volume. Nonetheless, here are a couple of thoughts. (1) Every statistical model has assumptions. Different models make different assumptions. R^2 equations "assume that the sample is obtained by simple random sampling at all levels" (Hox, 2010, p. 73). That is clearly not true here. This violated assumption contributes to the negative R^2 at level 2. (2) In the Monopoly dataset, the distribution of scores on the two level-1 predictors – the presence or absence of a hotel, and the number of guesthouses – are closely comparable across the different sides of the board. This would not happen if properties, neighborhoods, and stages of development were all sampled from larger populations at each level. Therefore, in this dataset the level-1 predictors are comparably distributed in each level-2 group. This also can lead to negative R^2 values at level 2 (Hox, 2010, p. 74). For more details see Hox (2010, pp. 72–74).

PRE and the Total Bucket

What to do? Snijders and Bosker (2012) recommend focusing on "the proportional reduction in error for predicting an individual outcome" (Snijders & Bosker, 2012, p. 111). This aligns with what is most typically meant when discussing R^2 in a monolevel regression. Their Eq. 7.3 defines a quantity, R^2_1, as follows.

> We define the explained proportion of variance at level one. This is based on how well we can predict the outcome Y_{ij} for a randomly drawn level-one unit i within a randomly drawn level-2 unit j . . . the level-one explained proportion of variance is defined as the proportional reduction in mean squared prediction error.
>
> (Snijders & Bosker, 2012, p. 112)

A simplified equation for level-1 R^2, adapted from their Eq. 7.3 (Snijders & Bosker, 2012, p. 112), appears here:

$$R^2_1 = 1 - \left(\frac{\text{Variance } \left(Y_{ij} - Y_{ij\,predicted}\right)}{\text{Variance } \left(Y_{ij}\right)} \right) \tag{Eq. 7.4}$$

Plugging in the numbers from Table 7.2 generates the "explained proportion of [outcome] variance at level one" (Snijders & Bosker, 2012, p. 112) for ANCOVA Model 4:

$$R^2_1 = 1 - \frac{73,056.82}{204,954.46} = 0.64 \qquad \text{(Eq. 7.5)}[9]$$

If you could look inside the bucket of total outcome variation, you would see that the predictors have removed about 2/3 of the water, leaving the bucket about a third full of residual, unexplained rent differences. See Figure 7.6.

How R^2 Works Depends on the Type of Outcome You Have

Calculating explained variance at specific levels pertains only to models where your outcome is a normally distributed continuous variable. If your outcome is *not* a normally distributed continuous variable, then calculating the explained variance becomes more complicated, as is true as well in single-level multiple regressions with binary, count, or multinomial outcomes. Part of the challenge arises because moving from a normally distributed continuous outcome variable to something else like a binary, count, or ordinal outcome variable allows multiple definitions of explained variance (Long, 1997, pp. 102–113). When working on those different types of outcomes in different datasets, I recommend relying on differences in values of BIC and AIC to decide when one model is "better" than another one. With some multilevel models, deviance tests also can be used for gauging which models better predict data (Snijders & Bosker, 2012, p. 97).

Figure 7.6   Remaining $(1 - R^2_1)$ total rent variation, about 1/3 of the initial volume.

Summary

Rent was predicted with a multilevel model (Table 7.2, Model 4), including two indicators of real estate development levels, n_house and hotel, allowing each development variable to have just one average impact, while simultaneously allowing each neighborhood its own level-2 rent residual. Such models can reveal neighborhood effects while controlling for compositional effects, but not the reverse. It is sometimes misunderstood that these models fail to fully control for between-neighborhood differences. To completely remove neighborhood outcome differences requires a different analysis, for example, with j-1 dummy variables for j groups (Table 7.2, Model 3). That approach, a fixed effects model, transforms *b* weights for level-1 predictors into indicators of only within-neighborhood impacts. Following Snijders and Bosker, a proportional reduction in error approach to level-1 R^2 was outlined.

Notes

1 Neighborhood effects means something specific in urban sociology. "Whether assuming social learning processes from significant others in the local context or an epidemic spread of [social] norms, social and spatial interdependence are at the core of most theoretical explanations of neighborhood effects" (Zangger, 2019, p. 1056). See also Sharkey and Faber (2014), Sampson et al. (2002), and Sampson (2012). The term is used more broadly here to indicate between-neighborhood dynamics reflected in significant between-neighborhood outcome variation.
2 Compositional effects means something more specific in urban sociology (Jencks & Mayer, 1990; Tienda, 1991). In this field, compositional effects "arise from the more static features of sociodemographic composition (e.g., race, class position)," which vary between neighborhoods (Sampson et al., 2002, p. 447).
3 See Allison (2009, pp. 2–3, chapter 1, online version):

> In a random effects model, the unobserved variables are assumed to be uncorrelated with (or, more strongly, statistically independent of) all observed variables. . . . In a fixed effects model, the unobserved variables are allowed to have any associations whatever with the observed variables (which turns out to be equivalent to treating the unobserved variables as fixed parameters). Unless you allow for such associations, you haven't really controlled for the effects of the unobserved variables.

> Perhaps more simply, the "key issue" with unobserved components or unobserved heterogeneity "is whether or not it is uncorrelated with the observed explanatory variables" (Wooldridge, 2002, p. 252).

4 "It is assumed here that the level-two residuals U_{0j} [for varying intercepts] and U_{ij} [for varying slopes] as well as the level-one residuals R_{ij} have mean 0, given the values of the explanatory variable X" (Snijders & Bosker, 2012, p. 75).
5 Of course, this also could be done on the fly as in Chapter 5.
6 Table generated using the etable command available in V. 17 of Stata.
7 For example, the variable 2.side corresponds to the properties between Jail and Free Parking. Choosing this variable, however, makes the constant uninterpretable (see lines 23–24).
8 It just so happens, given the Monopoly data structure, that neighborhood rent effects are the same, 18.78%, whether controlling for development or not. With real datasets, gross and net level-2 outcome impacts are likely to differ.
9 73,056.82 = 40,120.58 + 32,936.24. The last two numbers are from Model 4, Table 7.2.

8　Third Multilevel Model

Do Neighborhoods Alter Hotel Rent Impacts?

Overview

This chapter takes many twisty turns. Here is an itinerary for the road trip. First stop: theory, including interactions, moderating effects, and cross-level interactions. What are they? The latter can prove crucial to testing and advancing multilevel theories. Second stop: operationalize the theoretical question. The crucial cross-level process highlighted here asks, does the rent impact of a hotel vary depending on the neighborhood where the property is located? Third stop: an outcome operationalization question with analytic and theoretical implications. Is it a good idea or a bad idea to transform the slightly non-normally distributed rent outcome variable? The next three stops dive into the doing. Fourth stop: model selection – deciding if the model allowing the level-1 impact to vary across contexts outperforms other models. Fifth stop: interpret findings, both statistical and graphical. The latter describes how varying impacts are operating in different neighborhoods. Sixth stop: as part of *routine due diligence*, check "under the hood." Fascinating findings prove problematic following careful checking. Finally, pause for the seventh and final stop: reflect. What are the implications for working with other datasets? With an adequate data source, how to further theory development?

First Stop: Theory

Cross-Level Interactions: Logic of Inquiry

When multilevel models first gained popularity in social science disciplines, researchers expressed excitement. Why? These models showed potential for clearly and compactly illuminating cross-level interactions. Cross-level interactions describe situations where *impacts* of a lower-level (e.g., level-1) predictor depend on a higher-level (e.g., level-2) context attribute. Investigating cross-level interactions involves the following questions: (1) Does the impact of a lower-level predictor depend significantly upon, that is, vary across, groups into which the lower-level units are clustered? Further, if the impact does vary, (2a)

DOI: 10.4324/9781003392682-8

how is that dependency organized? Further, (2b) is it more than random noise? Finally, if statistically significant and sensibly organized, (3) does that dependency link *statistically* to a *theoretically based interaction term* that includes both the level-1 predictor with varying impact and a specific level-2 predictor? Such a linkage enhances the explanatory power of the model.

Note the three-step logic of inquiry: (1) Show that a lower-level predictor's impact varies. (2) Establish that the variation is more than random noise. (3) Then improve the overall model by including a theoretically based interaction term combining the varying-impact, lower-level predictor with a higher-level predictor linked to that varying impact. There should be a clear theoretical rationale for this cross-level dynamic. Such cross-level dynamics prove crucial for many core theoretical and practical questions in a wide range of social science disciplines.

Key Cross-Level Interaction Investigated Here

This chapter launches, but does not complete, an investigation into a specific cross-level theoretical dynamic. Does the rent impact of a hotel depend on the side of the board – the neighborhood – where the hotel is built? This type of multilevel model is called a random-coefficients regression model; a coefficient – here, hotel rent impact – can vary randomly across neighborhoods.

Cross-Level Interactions: Examples and Theoretical Components

Single-Level Interactions

Recall what an interaction effect is in a single-level regression model with two predictors, A and B. A significant interaction effect is observed if the population slope of predictor A varies depending on levels of predictor B, or vice versa (Blalock, 1979, p. 420).

AKA Moderator Effects

Equivalently, the effect of one predictor adjusts or moderates the impact of the other predictor involved in the significant interaction effect. This is a moderator effect (Mackinnon & Pirlott, 2015). Do not confuse it with a mediating effect (Baron & Kenny, 1986).

Cross-level Interactions Defined

An interaction effect, or moderator effect, becomes a *cross-level interaction* if "it involves explanatory variables from different levels" (Hox, 2010, p. 20).

This label applies as well to longitudinal data structures with repeated observations over time (Chapter 9).

Cross-level Interactions Over Space: Actual Examples

Turning to my disciplinary interests, cross-level interactions play important roles in numerous criminological theories, including, for example, models of offending (Wilcox et al., 2003) and victimization (Miethe & Meier, 1994). Examples also appear in the criminal legal system. (1) Some judges – but not others – penalize defendants more harshly at sentencing if those defendants opt to go to trial but end up being found guilty (Ulmer & Bradley, 2006). (2) The effects of defendant race on whether or not the death penalty is pursued can depend upon the county where the case is located (Paternoster et al., 2004). Additional examples abound, for example, in educational psychology (Hox et al., 2018, pp. 16–19) and environmental psychology (Lockwood et al., 2021).

Developing the Supporting Theoretical Dynamics

It is one thing to program analyses permitting a level-1 predictor to have varying impacts across different level-2 units. It is harder specifying the theoretical underpinnings. Three specifications are key. (1) *Theoretically* which predictor should have varying impacts and why? (2) *Theoretically*, which specific grouping variable should alter whether the level-1 predictor has stronger or weaker impacts on the outcome? Further, (3) what is the responsible mechanism?

Not surprisingly then, given the rigorous requirements, cross-level interaction theorizing seems underdeveloped in many areas of social science inquiry. Theorizing about main effects of persons, locations, groupings, or time, or about interaction effects involving predictors all at the same level, seems to predominate.

> Multilevel problems must be explained by multilevel theories, an area that seems undeveloped compared to the advances made in modeling and computing machinery . . . if there are effects of the social context on individuals, these effects must be mediated by intervening processes that depend on characteristics of the social context. When the number of variables at the different levels is large, there are an enormous number of possible cross-level interactions. Ideally, a multilevel theory should specify which variables belong to which level, and which direct effects and cross-level interaction effects can be expected. Cross-level interactions between the individual and the context level require the specification of processes

within individuals that cause those individuals to be differentially influenced by certain aspects of the context.

(Hox, 2010, p. 7)

In effect, Hox (2010) is saying that if cross-level interactions are to make sense, substantial theoretical requirements must be met. Meeting these requirements may require extending theories beyond their current boundaries. You may be working, as the late Shel Silverstein (1974/2004, p. 89) put it, "at the edge of the world" where the "sidewalk" – your theory – *does* end.

Supporting Theoretical Dynamics for the Hotel Example

To extend rather than run out of theoretical sidewalk here, consider the following rationale supporting the hypothesis that hotels charge higher rents in higher SES neighborhoods.

Scholarship in tourism economics applies the idea of "willingness to pay" or WTP for specific attributes of potential vacation destinations. For example, in one recent study enrolling residents of Northern Spain, "individuals are willing to pay, on average, about €120 for lodging at a four-star hotel relative to an apartment" (Boto-Garcia et al., 2022, p. 363). Researchers also observed heterogeneity in preferences, with individuals' income levels being one factor shaping preferences and price sensitivity.

Variations in WTP, within and between different preference classes of early 20th century vacationers seeking to rent in Atlantic City, could help explain why hotel rent impacts might be larger in higher SES neighborhoods. Higher income visitors may value more highly, and thus be willing to pay more, for better-situated hotels. Several reasons might drive the willingness. The quality of the accommodation would be better. Visitors would find more popular entertainment venues nearby. Finally, in the pre-air-conditioning era, access to afternoon, onshore cooling breezes would be better, as would access to the Boardwalk itself.

Street names in the real Atlantic City, and appearing on the fourth side of the Monopoly board, all would have had these advantages in the first half of the 20th century. In contrast, street names in the real Atlantic City and appearing on the first side of the Monopoly board would have had none of these advantages.

In short, variations in willingness to pay among certain segments of 1920s and 1930s hotel patrons, tied to specific features of the establishments and their location, may be the theoretical process driving the hypothesized cross-level interaction effect tested here.

A Big Idea Expressed Two Different Ways

Here is the big idea driving random-coefficients regression with cross-level interactions. It is one idea (Baumer & Arnio, 2012), just phrased differently depending on whether your units are clustered by space or by time (Chapter 9).

- Spatial variation: for cross-sectional clustered data, each lower-level predictor can potentially have impacts that depend upon the group into which the lower-level units are clustered. The cross-level interaction links varying impacts of the lower-level predictor to scores on a group attribute.
- Temporal variation: for longitudinal data, with multiple observations over time for each unit, each of the latter can chart its own individual pathway of outcome scores over time (Raudenbush, 2005). The impacts of time can vary across the units observed: for example, an individual, an organization, or a spatial unit like a neighborhood or a city. The cross-level interaction links varying impacts of time to an attribute of the units repeatedly observed.

Second Stop: Operationalize the Theoretical Question

Landing on Boardwalk with a hotel costs $2,000 in 1935 dollars. Landing on a hotel-encumbered green property or Park Place exacts almost the same penalty. By contrast, landing on a purple property with a hotel proves less painful. Baltic with a hotel costs $450 in 1935 dollars. This leads to the following question:

- Is the impact of a hotel on rent *bigger* on *some* sides of the board as compared to others?

Restating the same question more formally:

- Does the rent impact of the level-1 predictor, the presence or absence of a hotel, *vary significantly* depending on the neighborhood – the side of the playing board – on which the property is located?

Relevant Equations

Chapter 7 presented the combined equation predicting rent (Y_{ij}, Eq. 7.1) for the ANCOVA model. If that ANCOVA model were broken down into equations at each level, the level-1 ANCOVA model would be:

$$Y_{ij} = \beta_{0j} + \beta_{1j}X_{1ij} + \beta_{2j}X_{2ij} + r_{ij} \qquad \text{(Eq. 8.1)}$$

Translation: individual rent values = the neighborhood average deviation from overall rent after controlling for development (β_{0j}); plus the net rent impact, for that neighborhood (β_{1j}), of the number of guesthouses (X_{1ij}); plus the net rent impact, for that neighborhood (β_{2j}), of the presence/absence of hotel (X_{2ij}); plus a within-neighborhood rent residual (r_{ij}).

Furthermore, the level-2 ANCOVA model would include the following three equations.

$$\beta_{0j} = \gamma_{00} + u_{0j} \tag{Eq. 8.2a}$$

Translation (Eq. 8.2a): Neighborhood *j*'s deviation from overall rent after controlling for development = overall adjusted rent mean, plus neighborhood *j*'s remaining average discrepancy between observed and predicted rent.

$$\beta_{1j} = \gamma_{10} \tag{Eq. 8.2b}$$

Translation (Eq. 8.2b): The net rent impact of number of guest houses, for neighborhood *j* = the average net rent impact of number of guest houses for all neighborhoods.

$$\beta_{2j} = \gamma_{20} \tag{Eq. 8.2c}$$

Translation (Eq. 8.2c): The net rent impact of a hotel being present, for neighborhood *j* = the average net rent impact of a hotel for all neighborhoods.

Now for the big leap.

In this new model, the random coefficients regression (RCR) model, group context can alter predicted net hotel rent impacts. Those impacts can now vary randomly across the four different sides of the playing board. The level-2 equation for β_{2j} (Eq. 8.2c) makes this model change by adding one new term, u_{2j}. The revised level-2 equation for net hotel rent impacts in the RCR model is:

$$\beta_{2j} = \gamma_{20} + u_{2j} \tag{Eq. 8.3}$$

Translation: the predicted net rent impact of hotel for neighborhood j (β_{2j}) = the average net rent impact of hotel for all neighborhoods (γ_{20}), *plus* the discrepancy (u_{2j}) between the predicted net hotel rent impact for neighborhood j and that overall average hotel rent impact. EB adjustments apply to these slope discrepancies and shrink them toward the average hotel slope. Each neighborhood ($n = 4$) has its own discrepancy between its β weight for hotel and the average β weight for hotel.

Illustrating the Key Equation With Specific Results

Although Monopoly RCR model results have not yet been presented, a graph illustrating each neighborhood's estimated varying hotel rent impact may help. EB adjusted hotel slopes (β_{2j}), for each neighborhood, appear in Figure 8.1.

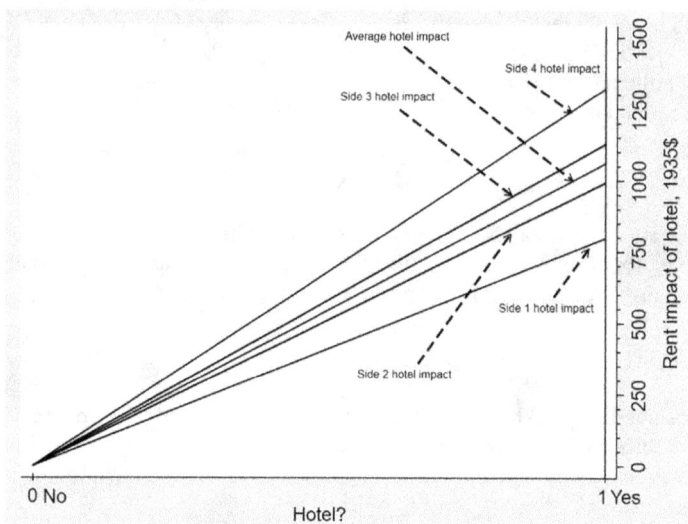

Figure 8.1 Net, EB-adjusted neighborhood-level hotel rent impacts, and overall hotel rent impact.

The absence ($X_2 = 0$) or presence ($X_2 = 1$) of the hotel predictor appears on the x-axis. The net hotel rent impact appears on the y-axis. Recall from undergraduate statistics: a *b* weight indicates "rise over run." As you "run" out one unit on the predictor, going on the horizontal axis from absence (0) to presence (1) of a hotel, how much does rent "rise" up the vertical axis? The average impact of a hotel, the average rise/run, equals $1,060.48 (Table 8.1, RCR model). For sides 3 and 4, the lines rise faster than the average rise/run. For sides 1 and 2, the lines rise more slowly than the average. Each of the four β_{2j} lines combines two elements: $\gamma_{20} + u_{2j}$.[1]

Restating the Central Question in Different Ways

Do net hotel rent impacts vary across neighborhoods, or are they essentially the same across neighborhoods? The central question can be framed in terms of competing models. Compared to the model with just one average net hotel rent impact, the ANCOVA model, does the model allowing net hotel rent impact to vary from neighborhood to neighborhood, the RCR model, do better?

Additional Model Features

Note the RCR model adds two additional parameters. Since these predicted net hotel rent impacts (β_{2j}s) can vary, they have a variance (τ_{22}). Further, the varying predicted net hotel rent impacts can covary with varying level-2 rent residuals (β_{0j}s). This last parameter of covariation gets close attention when looking under the hood at RCR model details.

A Simpler Approach?

You may wonder: is there a simpler approach? Why not just do a separate multiple regression, one for properties on each side of the board, and compare the hotel *b* weights from the different regression models?

The concern here is this. Those four independent multiple regressions would not really be independent. The different regressions all come from the same dataset and thus are not independent. Multilevel models anticipate and factor in that interrelatedness across the different groups. Stated more directly, these RCR models will make EB adjustments to deviations in predicted net hotel rent impacts across the four sides of the board (u_{2j} values), based on features of *all* the data, in the same way EB adjustments to level-2 intercepts and residuals were made (Raudenbush & Bryk, 2002, pp. 45–46). The adjustments shrink the slope deviations toward the average slope.

Monopoly Data for RCR Varying Impacts Model: Flaws When Using These Monopoly Data to Illustrate Random Coefficients Regression, but Pedagogical Advantages

The Monopoly rent data have some warts when used for multilevel models. For the RCR model, as you will witness on the sixth stop, one of these flaws proves problematic.

When illustrating the random coefficients regression model, Monopoly data violate a key assumption of multilevel models. These models assume that the *u* parameters (u_{0j}, u_{2j}) "are multivariate normally distributed" (Raudenbush & Bryk, 2002, p. 76). With just four sides of the board, this assumption is not met.

A second *potential* concern is multicollinearity between the *u* parameters (u_{0j}, u_{2j}). "These two group effects will usually not be independent, but correlated" (Snijders & Bosker, 2012, p. 75). Severe multicollinearity among predictors – the predictors correlating much too strongly with one another – creates analytic concerns as well as conceptual indistinguishability (Blalock, 1963). Multicollinearity among mixed-model estimated parameters can prove troublesome as well (Shieh & Fouladi, 2003). Such trouble seems more likely to surface with a small number of groups. What happens if the estimates of the *u* parameters (u_{0j}, u_{2j}) are *too* strongly correlated? Stay tuned.

Despite these dataset disadvantages, the small number of groups in this dataset is a pedagogical advantage. With four groups, you can learn in detail what is happening with each individual group. See Figure 8.1, for example. With many groups, it is often hard to see such details about what is happening.

With multilevel models of a certain level of complexity, like RCR models, these Monopoly data are best viewed as a set of training data, albeit a set allowing you to really dig into what these models are doing statistically and theoretically. Just keep their limitations in mind. Even more importantly, these limitations notwithstanding, the steps in the multilevel model investigatory process outlined here are *exactly* the ones to use regardless of data simplicity or complexity.

Third Stop: Transform the Outcome Variable?

On this stop, consider an operational question with theory and policy implications. In the US version of Monopoly, rent is in dollars. Price data often spread out more at higher values. Here, as already seen (Figure 5.3), rent interquartile ranges grow larger in higher SES neighborhoods. This means rent has a positively skewed distribution. Too much skew violates an assumption of the model: a normally distributed outcome variable.

The histogram of the rent variable appears in Figure 8.2. The skewness statistic = .86. This suggests a distribution that is "moderately skew"; if the

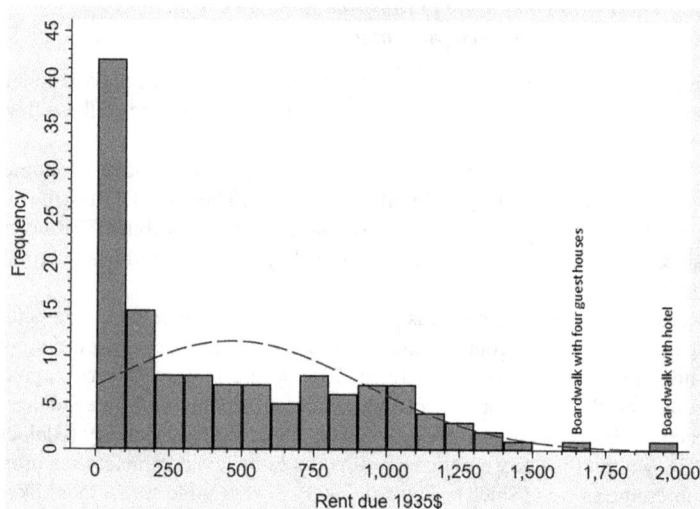

Figure 8.2 Distribution of rent, 1935$, with normal curve superimposed.

"skewness [statistic is] greater than 1 in absolute value," the distribution would be "highly skew[ed]" (Bulmer, 1967, p. 63). In short, although the distribution is not symmetrical, it is not wildly non-normal or "highly skew[ed]." In this situation, some might recommend a natural logarithmic transformation of rent values.

Nonetheless, empirical, practical, and theoretical reasons recommend against doing that. First, the empirical. A log transform does not improve the skewness statistic much; skew $= -.74$ after the natural log transform, still suggesting a "moderately skew[ed]" variable. Even though a "logarithmic transformation can produce data that are substantially more symmetric," it does not do so here (Hannon & Knapp, 2003, p. 1429). Further, even after transformation, the variances are still heterogeneous. See the log output file for details. Of course, one could explore a number of different transformations, using the Stata command gladder, to learn if any would create a normally distributed outcome.

Second, a practical reason. A transformed outcome variable loses its natural metric, dollars. Consequently, results will be more challenging for some audiences to absorb. An outcome lacking readily grasped units of measurement creates an additional barrier to clearly communicating model results, especially with policy-oriented audiences.

Finally, theoretical reasons argue against transforming the rent variable. Hannon and Knapp (2003, p. 1427)

> argue that the problems frequently corrected by logarithmic transformation of the dependent variable (mainly outlying influential observations and nonconstant error variance) can and should be corrected by other means when a primary concern of the analyses is the theoretically motivated assessment of nonlinear relationships or interaction effects.

Here, the "primary concern" is the cross-level interaction between hotel impact and neighborhood context. As Figure 8.1 shows, the relationship is nonlinear in that the increase in hotel rent impact is not uniform as one progresses around the board. The net hotel rent impact difference going from the first to the second side ($195.52), and from the third to the fourth side ($193.75), is greater than the shift going from the second to the third side of the board ($134.96). This argues against transforming this outcome in this particular case here.

Pulling the lens back, consider some broader issues about whether to transform an outcome variable. Tukey's (1957, p. 602) points, addressing either a predictor or an outcome variable, provide helpful guidance. He suggested that a decision to transform could be driven by any of three primary reasons: "[1] providing approximations for theoretical purposes [2] or general convenience; [or for] . . . [3] bending the data nearer . . . the assumptions underlying conventional analyses."

Turning back to the case here, the log transform does not help with Tukey's reason [3]; the degree of non-normality is similar before and after the transform. It does not help with Tukey's reason [2]; in fact, it makes the analysis less convenient because readily understood outcome units have been rubbed out by the transform. And finally, turning to Tukey's reason [1], the transform works *against* the key theoretical purpose here, potentially obscuring the central interaction effect (Hannon & Knapp, 2003).

The takeaway: consider carefully before transforming the outcome variable. Contemplate practical, theoretical, and analytic advantages and disadvantages.

Fourth Stop: Preliminaries, Then Model Selection

Descriptive Statistics

Examine the descriptive statistics for predictors and outcome. Look at these two ways: for the entire dataset and by group.

Verifying Predictor-Variable Variation in Each Group

When looking by group, be especially alert. Do the data contain sufficient variation on this hotel predictor variable *in each group*? Cross tabbing (see do file for this chapter) the variable whose impacts will be varying, by side of the board, shows five or six observations with hotels present. In each neighborhood, observations with hotels appear in one-sixth (16.7%) of the records.

Why worry about this? Game designers constructed these data, and one result was the distribution of the hotel variable. Since you have played this game, you already know that each property deed can have a hotel.

Nevertheless, check closely when working with real observations. You do not want to run RCR models where there is either *no* variation on a predictor or *very little* variation on a predictor, *within* one of your level-2 groups. Here is why.

Suppose you had a side of the board with no hotels in any of the observations. If conducting a monolevel regression for just that one group of observations, the model could not run. The hotel predictor would be zero for all records. No variation in the predictor, no regression line built. With a multilevel RCR model, when the program sees a group with no variation for a predictor variable with varying impacts in the model, it drops that group from the analysis. Therefore, in the output file, carefully examine the information provided ahead of the main results. These details show how many cases were analyzed, how many groups, and how many cases per group. Look for cases or groups dropping out.

A different kind of problem arises in a group with just one or two observations where `hotel` = 1. Imagine a hotel possible for only one property on the first side of the board (`sidezero` = 0). When the multilevel RCR model estimates an initial slope for that side of the board, the *b* weight for net hotel rent impact is based on 29 records where `hotel` = 0 and just one record where `hotel` = 1. Consequently, for this this side of the board, it is not clear whether the *b* weight reflects net hotel rent impact in this group or, instead, something unique to that particular property's hotel. This is another reason to examine closely distributions of *each* predictor in *each* level-2 group. In short, there should be at least a decent fraction of cases at *each* level of the independent variable in *each* of your level-2 groups.

What is a decent fraction? There is no simple answer. Five percent might be fine if based on at least 1,000 observations in each level-2 group. You have to figure this out as you go. If the needed examination becomes tedious with many level-2 groups, use summarizing graphical displays: box-and-whisker plots or stem-and-leaf plots (Tukey, 1977). They can help you quickly spot groups with no or minimal variation on key predictors.

This same checking protocol applies when doing an RCR with a three-level model. For example, imagine survey respondents within neighborhoods within cities. A three-level model might allow one or more level-2, neighborhood-level predictors to have varying impacts across different level-3 groups (cities). At the front end, verify a sensible distribution for each of these key level-2 predictors – a decent fraction at each value of the predictor – in each level-3 group.

Getting the Pieces You Need for Model Selection

Retain and report the results of your RCR model if, and only if, it does a better job explaining the outcome than the preceding, simpler model, the ANCOVA model; and you are convinced results are sound after carefully checking under the hood. Deciding if the RCR model is better requires assembling different bits of information. More specifically, (a) a likelihood ratio (LR) χ^2 test comparing the two competing models and (b) the size of differences in model-fit-while-controlling-for-model-complexity indicators when the two models are contrasted; and, if applicable, (c) factoring in relevant practical or policy study purposes.[2]

ANOVA Model

First, run the ANOVA model. This generates key baseline indicators – the initial variances needed for later calculations, the crucial intraclass correlation, and the initial AIC and BIC values. Most importantly, it justifies using a multilevel model (Chapter 6).

Building Towards a Model With Cross-level Interactions

When allowing slopes to vary, matters complicate quickly. Consider these general suggestions (Raudenbush & Bryk, 2002) about in-between steps while working toward an RCR model that includes a specific cross-level interaction.

1. Decide theoretically which level-1 fixed effects to include in your model. Include them. Assess the model and parameter estimates.
2. Decide theoretically which level-2 fixed effects (Chapter 10) to include in the model. Include them. Assess.
3. While including groups of fixed effects, decide on the centering approach for each group (Chapter 10).
4. Decide *theoretically* whether to include a specific predictor or a specific set of predictors. Do *not* drop specific variables or blocks of variables if they underperform (Berk et al., 2009).
5. Run corresponding monolevel models.
6. For each new multilevel model – the ANOVA, the ANCOVA with level-1 predictors, the ANCOVA with level-1 and level-2 predictors – tell the reader whether each progressively more elaborate model provides a better fit with the data.
7. With all fixed effects figured out, go to work on random effects. This might involve, for example, a level-1 predictor with varying impacts across level-2 groups. Think carefully not only about each random effect but also about potential relationships between different random effects. For each random effect, as done for each fixed effect, provide an accompanying theoretical rationale.
8. Demonstrate empirically that the model where a specific level-1 predictor has varying impacts does better than the model without that variation.
9. Check carefully under the hood for potential modeling problems *even if* the RCR looks like the preferred model.
10. Develop and state the theoretical rationale focusing on a *specific* cross-level interaction effect. This effect involves both the level-1 predictor whose impacts are allowed to vary and a *specific* level-2 predictor. Showing that the level-1 predictor has differential impacts is just the first step in investigating a cross-level interaction. It is not yet clear *why* its impact varies. Stated differently, what is the key level-2 attribute shaping that differential impact of the level-1 predictor? A stated theoretical rationale (a) provides the why, describing the specific theoretical moderating process(es) involved; and (b) points to a specific level-2 attribute, captured with a specific level-2 predictor, involved in the specified moderating theoretical process(es).
11. Then, construct the cross-level interaction effect(s), add to the model, and see if the model does better. More specifically, (a) the interaction term should prove significant, and (b) entering that term should noticeably

reduce the residual variation of the slopes of the variable with differential impacts. Regrettably, Monopoly dataset limitations will not allow illustrating this last step.

Model Selection: Is the RCR Better Than the ANCOVA?

Two approaches help decide if the RCR model is better than the ANCOVA model. The first uses a LR χ^2 test comparing the differences across the two models and tests its significance. A second approach uses two "measures of information" (Long, 1997, p. 109), the Akaike Information Criterion (AIC) and the Bayesian Information Criterion (BIC). Some background on each follows before moving on to the specific test results generated here.

Background on Likelihood-Ratio Test[3]

The likelihood-ratio test, Stata procedure lrtest, can compare whether random intercepts are needed (Rabe-Hesketh & Skrondal, 2012a, pp. 88–89) and whether random slopes for a predictor are needed (Rabe-Hesketh & Skrondal, 2012a, pp. 88–89, 197–198). Here, the null hypothesis tested is that the variance of the slope of the level-1 predictor is zero. "The null hypothesis also implies" that the covariation between the random intercepts and the random slopes in question is zero "because a variable that does not vary also does not vary with other variables" (Rabe-Hesketh & Skrondal, 2012a, p. 197). Here, the particular new variance components introduced are two: (1) the variance of the slopes reflecting different net rent impacts for hotel and (2) the covariance between the varying hotel slopes and the level-2 residuals.

Due to technical complexities (Rabe-Hesketh & Skrondal, 2012a, pp. 197–198), the reported significance level accompanying the resulting lrtest χ^2 value is not the correct. Nonetheless, "the correct *p*-value can simply be obtained by dividing the naïve *p*-value based on the χ^2 by 2" (Rabe-Hesketh & Skrondal, 2012a, p. 198).

A significant-after-adjustment lrtest χ^2 means reject the idea that the variation in the random slopes for the predictor is zero. Retain the random slopes for the level-1 predictor.[4]

Background on BIC and AIC

The command estat ic also generates two additional numbers: AIC and BIC. When AIC and BIC values are compared across models, differences in values answer this question: does one model better fit the data than the other model while controlling for differing levels of model complexity? The more complex model is penalized because it uses more parameters to fit the data.

Here is the theoretical thinking about penalizing for increasing model complexity. Models can always explain more outcome variation by adding more features: more predictors, or as done here, more parameters like a variance and a covariance for a level-1 predictor slope. Nevertheless, models that are more complex stray further from a sought-after value in theory: parsimony. "Parsimony, the conciseness and abstractness of a set of concepts and propositions [in a theory], is also a desirable characteristic in a scientific theory" (Akers & Sellers, 2012, p. 5). All else equal, prefer the simpler model, accepting the more complex one only if the gains in model-predicted fit to the data are worth it. The BIC statistic puts a value on model-fit-to-data-while-controlling-for-model-complexity (Long, 1997, pp. 110–112; Raftery, 1995a, 1995b). The AIC, or Akaike Information Criterion statistic (Akaike, 1974; Burnham & Anderson, 1998), does this as well, albeit framing the matter in a slightly different way (Vrieze, 2012; Yang, 2005). Regardless of which one is examined, these information-theoretical statistics prove especially useful when working with generalized linear models involving binary, count, multinomial, or ordinal outcome variables, and comparing competing models (Long, 1997, pp. 110–112).

To choose one model over the other, examine the size of the differences in the AIC or BIC statistic. With each pairwise comparison, calculate a difference.

If the difference is large enough, and goes in the right direction – smaller is better, indicating less lack of fit – it means that one model provides a better fit-controlling-for-model-complexity, and should be selected.

For the BIC statistic, the absolute differences may provide "weak" (difference = 0–2), "positive" (2–6), "strong" (6–10), or "very strong" (> 10) evidence that one model does better than another (Long, 1997, p. 112). Ideally, if the lrtest χ^2 shows a significant difference, the associated BIC and AIC statistics should each also suggest at least "positive" evidence in favor of the same model.

Understanding Model Selection Using lrtest: Needed Steps

The Stata do file for this analysis follows these steps:

1. Run the ANOVA (Chapter 6) model. Store estimates, named ANOVA.
2. Run the ANCOVA (Chapter 7) model. Store estimates, named ANCOVA.
3. Run the random coefficients regression (RCR) model.[5] It includes the same two fixed effects as the ANCOVA model, guesthouses, and hotels. The only difference is that net hotel rent impacts vary by neighborhood or side of the board. Store estimates, named RCR.
4. Invoke the lrtest χ^2 test comparing the two sets of stored model results, ANCOVA and RCR.[6]
5. Having decided on the preferred model, save predicted scores, including predicted slopes.

Understanding Model Selection: Obtaining BIC and AIC
Differences

Following the ANCOVA model, and again following the RCR model, issue the `estat ic` request. That produces log likelihood, AIC, and BIC values for each model.

Do the sizes of the AIC and BIC differences also agree with the results of `lrtest`? AICs and BICs capture *lack* of model-to-data fit controlling for model complexity. So smaller is better. Putting the simpler model first, and subtracting, produces the results shown here.

Model	AIC	BIC
ANCOVA	1,772.57	1,786.98
RCR	1,755.88	1,776.06
Difference	16.69	10.92

The BIC difference is greater than 10, providing "very strong" evidence the RCR model is preferred to the ANCOVA model. In sum, AIC and BIC differences and LR test results all suggest the RCR model is preferred over the ANCOVA model.

Fifth Stop: Interpreting Findings

Main Table of Results

Table 8.1 displays results of the preferred RCR model, along with those from the ANOVA and the ANCOVA models for comparison. Cross-reference lines in the table with lines in the `log` output file. Let's review.

In the ANCOVA and RCR models, the predicted b weight for n_house (Table 8.1, lines 1–4) is identical. The standard error is slightly different.

Turning to `hotel` (lines 5–8), its b weight is nearly identical in the ANCOVA and RCR models. Notice, however, that the standard error for the b weight more than doubles in the RCR model.

The level-2 residual variance (line 11) and the level-1 residual variance (line 17) each appear somewhat lower in the RCR as compared to the ANCOVA model.[7]

Since the level-2 residuals and the hotel slope deviations from the average hotel slope can correlate with each other, this creates a covariance (line 15). That covariance will be revisited later under "Digging deeper."

Table 8.1 Predicting rent: Null model (ANOVA), analysis of covariance (ANCOVA), and random coefficients regression (RCR) models

	Model	ANOVA	ANCOVA	RCR
	Predictor			
1	N of houses present		$215.786	$215.786
2			($12.236)	($11.264)
3			17.636	19.157
4			$p < .001$	$p < .001$
5	Hotel present (1) or not (0)		$1,060.518	$1,060.478
6			($48.942)	($106.585)
7			21.669	9.950
8			$p < .001$	$p < .001$
9	Intercept	$469.124	−$67.265	−$67.371
10		($100.569)	($104.549)	($88.852)
	Random-effects parameters			
11	var(_cons)	$35,277.262	$40,120.580	$28,528.900
12		($28,910.565)	($29,137.704)	($20,942.846)
13	var(hotel)			$37,315.355
14				($30,718.552)
15	cov(hotel,_cons)			$32,627.679
16				($23,918.921)
17	var(e)	$169,677.210	$32,936.236	$27,913.974
18		($21,216.497)	($4,117.279)	($3,489.403)
	Model parameters			
19	N observations	132	132	132
20	Log likelihood	−986.17	−881.28	−870.94
21	AIC	1978.33	1772.56	1755.88
22	BIC	1986.98	1786.98	1776.06
23	Wald χ^2 model test	.	531.21	403.43
24	Model test p-value	.	$p < .001$	$p < .001$
25	N RE parameters	2.00	2.00	4.00
26	N variances/ covariances	2.00	2.00	3.00

Note: Outcome is rent due in 1935$. Standard errors in parentheses. var(hotel) = variance of varying b weights for hotel rental impact. var(_cons) = level-2 residual variance. var(e) = level-1 residual variance.

Turning to the overall model, the Wald χ^2 test for the entire model is still significant (lines 23–24). This test appears just *above* the main table of results in the `log` output file.

Not shown in Table 8.1, but just *below* the main output table of results in the `log` file, is an LR χ^2 test. The line reads as follows:

```
LR test vs. linear model: chi2(3) = 105.28 Prob >
chi2 = 0.0000
```

Residual variation in level-2 intercepts remains significant. Additional, theoretically noteworthy between-neighborhood rent variation remains to be explained.

Digging Deeper

Which Net Hotel Rent Impacts Are Above or Below the Average Net Hotel Rent Impact?

To examine variations in `hotel` slopes, they must be built first. Construct them in post-estimation using `predict`. This parallels constructing level-2 residuals in earlier models.

A couple of comments about the relevant section of `do` file code for chapter **8**. There are now two random effects to be predicted: the neighborhood deviation from the average slope for `hotel` and the neighborhood rent residual. Stata generates two new variables from one stub name. Provide the beginning of the variable name, the stub, followed by an asterisk.

Be extremely careful here. It is easy to confuse which variable corresponds to which random effect. Stata generates the random effects in the order that they appear in the random-effects part of the output table in the log file. The first variable generated will be for the hotel random effect. Always look closely at how these variables are labeled using `describe` after creating them.

The random-effects variable for `hotel` only reflects *deviations* around the average impact. The online program also constructs the neighborhood-level predicted net `hotel` rent impact, whose results were graphed in Figure 8.1. The deviations in `hotel` slope were simply added to the average hotel slope.

To examine significant differences between neighborhood impacts in hotel net rent impacts, the online code constructs a caterpillar plot using `collapse` and `sebarr`. The resulting plot, including 95% confidence intervals, appears in Figure 8.3. The four confidence intervals do not overlap. Thus, for each of the four sides of the board, net hotel impacts differ

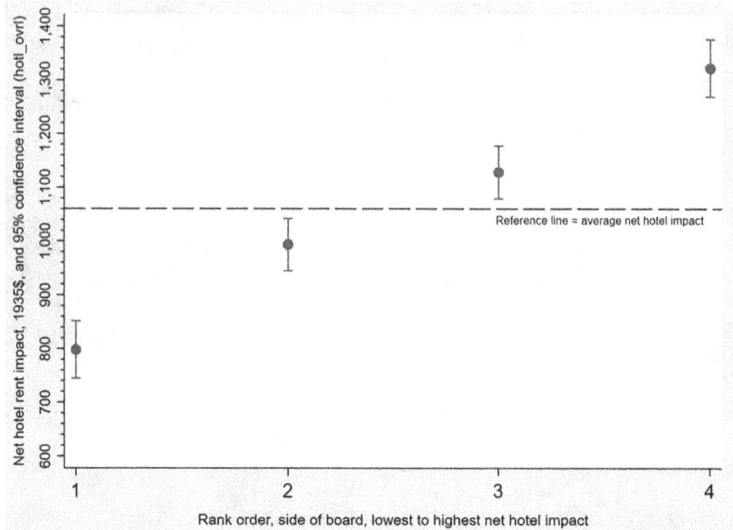

Figure 8.3 Caterpillar plot showing variations in net hotel rent impacts by side of the board, with 95% confidence intervals.

significantly from one another, increasing significantly each time you turn a corner on the board.

Recall the question posed at the outset. Does `hotel` have a significantly stronger net rent impact in higher SES neighborhoods? Decode the caterpillar plot for answers to the following specific questions. (1) Do any particular neighborhoods have a hotel rent impact significantly above the average impact? (2) Do any particular neighborhoods have a hotel rent impact significantly below the average hotel rent impact? (3) Do any specific neighborhoods differ significantly from any other specific neighborhoods in terms of hotel rent impact?[8]

Sixth Stop: Routine Due Diligence, Checking Under the Hood of Your Model

Routine Diagnostics: Predicted Scores and Residual Scores

Residual analyses should always be a routine part of checking under the hood of your multilevel model (Hox, 2010, pp. 24–28). Although not discussed here, the online program provides some of the standard residual model diagnostic plots needed.

The Relationship Between Level-2 Rent Residuals and Level-2 Hotel Slope Deviations

The RCR model has two random effects, and they correlate with one another: remaining neighborhood-level average rent residuals (u_{0j}) and neighborhood-level deviations in net hotel rent impact (u_{2j}). The main table of results [Table 8.1, line 15, `cov(hotel, _cons)`] includes a number describing how much the two random effects correlate with one another, expressed as a covariance number. What happens if that number is expressed as a correlation? Rerun the model, but use the stddeviations option.

```
mixed rent n_house hotel ||sidezero:hotel, ///
      cov(unstructured) ///
      stddeviations
```

See Table 8.2. The variations in level-2 `hotel` slope discrepancies from the average `hotel` *b* weight (`sd(hotel)`), level-2 mean rent residuals (`sd(_cons)`), and level-1 residuals (`sd(Residual)`) are displayed using standard deviations rather than variances. Most crucially, look at the correlation between level-2 mean rent residuals and level-2 `hotel` slope discrepancies (`corr(hotel, _cons)`). The correlation is essentially 1: .9999997. The two random effects parameters are almost identical with one another.

Yes, the program runs. Yes, the program outputs seemingly sensible estimates. But if two model parameters correlate almost perfectly, it is fair to ask if the two underlying ideas represented, level-2 residual rent variation, and level-2 `hotel` rent impact discrepancies from the average `hotel` impact, can be separated conceptually *with this dataset*. Indicators operationalize underlying concepts in a model (Taylor, 1994, p. 41). If "a given indicator is attached to more than one concept" that creates a situation of "semantic ambiguity" where "one fact means several things at once" (Abbott, 1997, pp. 361–362). That ambiguity is seen here. An earlier clue to this concern surfaced in

Table 8.2 Random effects portion for RCR model with stddeviations option

Random-effects parameters	Estimate	Std. err.	[95% conf. interval]	
sidezero: Unstructured				
sd(hotel)	193.1718	79.511	86.21502	432.8173
sd(_cons)	168.905	61.9959	82.26446	346.795
corr(hotel, _cons)	0.9999997	0.00013	−1.000	1.000
sd(Residual)	167.0748	10.4426	147.8115	188.8484
LR test vs. linear model: chi2(3) = 105.28	Prob > chi2 = 0.0000			

Note: Reproduced as shown in Chapter 8 log file.

Table 8.1, line 6. The standard error for the `hotel` *b* weight roughly doubled when going from the ANCOVA to the RCR model (Table 8.1, line 6).

Consider this question of whether to trust the RCR results at two levels. In the context of this specific dataset, with only four neighborhoods, such a problem is foreseeable. On the other hand, thinking beyond this dataset, a problem with highly collinear parameter estimates in an RCR model can easily crop up even in a dataset with many more level-2 groupings than seen here.

The Takeaway Lesson

All three metrics considered – the `lrtest` and the AIC and BIC differences – point to the RCR model as better than the ANCOVA model. At the same time, the RCR model has an extremely important limitation: two different estimated model parameters may, essentially, be the same thing.[9] This creates a conceptual conundrum. If the estimated parameters are essentially indistinguishable, then, *theoretically, the two underlying constructs are essentially indistinguishable as well*, at least when estimated using this dataset.

What to do?
My suggestion and the accompanying rationale is as follows. The suggestion assumes you are working with a real dataset; intend to publish scholarly work in a refereed article, scholarly book, book chapter, or thesis or dissertation; and are confronted with an RCR model with two strongly collinear random effects parameters.

I suggest stick with and present the ANCOVA model results.

Why?
Presenting the RCR results requires (1) being honest about what is happening under the hood, which (2) in turn requires wrapping the RCR results in so many spools of caution tape in the limitations section of an article that the strength of the entire scholarly contribution could be questioned. Most crucially, however, (3) with this dataset the distinct parameters in the RCR results just cannot align with distinct constructs in the underlying theory. The model, with this dataset, is not testing the theory specified.

Perhaps the most important takeaway lesson for RCR models is simply this: dig deep. Understand fully what different model parameters are showing, and crucially, how they link together.

Finally, there is also a takeaway lesson for social science research and researchers generally. Areas within psychology, including social psychology for example, are in a replication crisis (Malich & Munafò, 2022). Concerns about the health of the social science investigation enterprise place increasing emphases on replication, reproducibility, and data sharing. In this climate, it behooves all of us to generate empirical scholarship that is robust, replicable and clearly aligning with underlying theoretical ideas. This is another reason to go with ANCOVA results rather than RCR results in a situation like this.

Seventh Stop: Reflect

Starting Question and Underlying Rationale

This chapter sought to illustrate the initial steps for investigating cross-level interactions with multilevel models. Random coefficient regression (RCR) models first observe varying impacts of a level-1 predictor in different level-2 groups. The second step involves specifying which specific level-2 attribute shapes those shifting impacts of the designated level-1 predictor.

The economic concept of willingness to pay, applied in current tourism research, could explain why some segments of Atlantic City hotel-using vacationers in the early 20th century were willing to pay higher rents to stay in better furnished hotels, closer to the ocean-side beach, cooling afternoon breezes, the boardwalk itself, and major entertainment venues.[10] Applying that rationale to the current dataset led to the hypothesis that hotel net rent impacts would be higher, particularly on the fourth side of the board, than elsewhere.

Led to This Finding

Multiple model selection decision-making tools indicated that the predictions from the RCR model allowing variations, by neighborhood, in net hotel rent impacts, did a better job of matching model predictions to observed rent data. Such results aligned with initial theoretical expectations.

But Closer Examination Revealed a Problem

Closer examination, however, showed a serious flaw with RCR model estimates. With these data, neighborhood variations in the hotel b weight appeared essentially identical to remaining neighborhood average rent differences. In short, the empirical test of the conceptual model failed to separate the central construct of interest, neighborhood variations in hotel rent impacts, from another model construct. Given such a model weakness, reporting of these flawed RCR results is not recommended.

Key Practical Takeaway

Even relatively simple multilevel models can harbor defects. Often those are spotted only after careful examination and diagnostics. Close model checking is key.

Key Theoretical Next Steps for a Cross-level Interaction Model of Neighborhood Differences in Hotel Rent Impacts

Find or build another dataset containing more neighborhoods and more indicators, including theoretically relevant level-2 attributes. Test an RCR model like the one shown here, but without flaws. An RCR model outperforming an ANCOVA model demonstrates *that* a cross-level dynamic is operative.

Demonstrating *how* that process is working, however, requires (1) building a specific cross-level interaction term involving both hotel presence/absence at level-1 and a specific neighborhood attribute at level-2; then (2) showing that this RCR model with the interaction term did better, using the kinds of model selection tools reviewed here, than the RCR model without the interaction term.

In essence, this is going to where the sidewalk, the theory, ends, and extending it, testing as you go.

Notes

1   The average predicted net hotel rent impact, plus the EB-adjusted discrepancies in hotel rent impact on each side of the playing board, generate the following values for predicted net hotel rent impact on each side of the board:

Side of board	Overall net hotel rent impact
1 Mediterranean ➔ Connecticut	$797.92
2 St. Charles Place ➔ New York	$993.44
3 Kentucky ➔ Marvin Gardens	$1,128.40
4 Pacific ➔ Boardwalk	$1,322.15

2   Differences in multilevel model explained variance are not relevant to this specific comparison. "It is not straightforward to define the coefficients of determination [including R^2_l] . . . for random coefficient models" so "removing the random coefficient(s) [is recommended] for the purpose of calculating the coefficient of determination because this will usually yield values that are close to the correct version" (Rabe-Hesketh & Skrondal, 2012a, p. 192).

3   This likelihood ratio test is *different* from the one that appears in the output immediately below the main table of fixed-effects and random-effects results. The one immediately below main results gauges the significance of remaining level-2 outcome variation. See Chapter 6.

4   "Unfortunately, there is no straightforward procedure available for testing *several* [level-1 predictor slope] variances simultaneously, unless the random effects are independent" (Rabe-Hesketh & Skrondal, 2012a, p. 198, emphasis added).

5   Code for running the model:

```
mixed rent n_house hotel ||sidezero:hotel ///
     , cov(unstructured)
```

6   The code is:

```
lrtest RCR ANCOVA
```

7 Do *not* compare coefficients of determination across these two models (Rabe-Hesketh & Skrondal, 2012a, p. 192).

8 The answers are Question 1 yes (3, 4); Question 2 yes (1, 2); Question 3 yes for every pairwise comparison.

9 Some might argue that the level-2 mean rent residuals (u_{0j}) do not represent an underlying concept. I respectfully disagree. They represent a concept, albeit a broad one: observed ecological rent variation arising from not-yet-assessed neighborhood factors. Yes, it is a diffuse concept, but as the fixed-effects model in Chapter 7 showed (Table 7.2, Model 3), that variation is sizable.

10 Of course, let us not forget that this is a toy dataset from a designed game. Therefore, this is also about Parker Brothers' game designers imitating economic life.

9 Longitudinal Data

Did Some Properties Develop Faster Than Others?

Setup and Purpose

Setup

This chapter illustrates how RCR models apply to longitudinal questions. The illustration requires data with repeated observations over time. Units repeatedly observed could be anything: people, organizations, neighborhoods, cities, or societies. Each different observation for each different unit is time stamped. The researcher knows the specific timeframe corresponding to each indicator. Time-stamped-observations-within-units are at level 1, and the units themselves – people, organizations, or neighborhoods – are at level 2.[1]

To drive this example of longitudinal use of multilevel models (Raudenbush, 2001), I attach to each individual rent value for each property a hypothetical year. The year indicates the point in time when each property attained a specific stage of real estate development, from no guesthouses to a hotel. Rent is still the outcome of interest, but with a twist. With time as a predictor, attention centers on the rate of rent change. Hypothetical year at level 1 is the only predictor of interest. Records are grouped differently in this chapter compared to previous ones. Here, individual rent observations, at level 1 ($n = 6$ per group), are grouped into specific property deeds ($n = 22$) at level 2.

Given the history of Atlantic City, New Jersey (Johnson, 2009), and the 1935 launch of Monopoly, the time frame selected for the hypothetical year variable was 1880–1930. In the dataset, the 1880 value for year is when each property starts out as completely undeveloped, with no guesthouses and no hotels. Each property ends up being completely developed, with a hotel, by no later than 1930. Mortgaging guesthouses or hotels is not allowed. Consequently, during this period each property's rent only could increase.

Purpose

The main purposes of the analysis are twofold. First, in an ANCOVA frame, what are the average predicted impacts of each additional hypothetical year

DOI: 10.4324/9781003392682-9

on rent? Second, in an RCR frame, did different properties chart different rent increase pathways through time?

Overview

Topics Covered

As in the last chapter, our sojourn makes seven stops.

First stop: theory. What does it mean theoretically for time to have varying impacts for individuals or, as here, properties? As in the last chapter, these theoretical questions involve cross-level interactions.

Second stop: operationalization. How are theoretical questions about differential temporal impacts translated into specific model parameters and specific tests of those parameters?

Diving into the doing, the third stop considers questions of model selection. Again, as in the past chapter, statistical tests compare the performance of the RCR versus ANCOVA model.

Fourth stop: interpret findings from the selected model.

Fifth stop: check under the hood of the model, as part of routine due diligence. Closer inspection of model results suggests a concern similar to the one seen in the last chapter. "Déjà vu all over again," as Yogi Berra would have said.

Sixth stop: if all else fails, look at the data. A graphical data display, with linear and curvilinear smoothing trends superimposed clarifies how choosing the RCR model over the ANCOVA model generates a misleading result when compared to displayed data patterns.

Seventh and final stop: reflect further on theory, and suggest the kind of property-level indicators needed to fully test a model that not only allows each property to chart its own "pathway through time" (Raudenbush, 2005) but also includes a cross-level interaction to help understand why different properties followed different pathways.

Two Broader Points to Bear in Mind

The broader scholarship applying multilevel models to longitudinal questions is enormous and wide-ranging (Raudenbush, 2001; Twisk, 2013). Here are just a couple examples. Considering changing delinquents' views of the law, do the views of some mature faster than the views of others (Kaiser & Reisig, 2017)? Considering neighborhoods, do violent crime rates change in response to collective efficacy at different rates over time (Hipp & Wickes, 2017)?

Further, the RCR multilevel model used here is just one of many available analytics suitable for longitudinal questions. Alternate analytics include, to mention just two, growth curve modeling (Duncan et al., 1999) and trajectory models (Haviland et al., 2007; Raudenbush, 2001, 2005; Weisburd et al.,

2004). Different analytics reflect different ways researchers can conceptualize the impacts of time (Raudenbush, 2001, 2005).

In short, this chapter simply opens the door to a vast storehouse of longitudinal questions and available analytic frameworks. Although the steps you take here inside the storehouse are modest, you will see how multilevel models approach time questions, some of the ways these models can go awry, and ways to respond as modeling concerns arise.

First Stop, Theory, Including Moderating Effects and Cross-Level Interactions

(1) The first theoretical question is just this: given the programmed values for the hypothetical year variable, what was the annual rate at which rent increased on these properties? Stated differently, how much did real estate development forces drive up rent prices on an annual basis?

(2) The second theoretical question examines temporal variations in the rate of annual rent increases. Were rents increasing at a steady, constant pace throughout the period? Or alternatively, were rent increases between 1880 and 1930 more likely in some particular segments of this period?

(3) The third theoretical question examines spatial variations in the rate of annual rent increases. It asks: did all different properties follow the same rate of development-driven rent increases? Or alternatively, did different properties in different places chart different pathways of annual rent increases? How the same versus different pathways idea is answered can have significant policy implications. An example considering immigration-driven changes in welfare views is discussed toward the end of the chapter.

(4) The fourth theoretical question follows up on the third, if and only if the individual pathways through time idea, the RCR model, is supported. What property-level factors moderate the stronger versus weaker impact of each passing year on rent increases? Conceptual analogs to this fourth question appear in urban research on neighborhood house price trajectories (Raymond et al., 2016). Further, research has linked urban house price shifts or neighborhood house price shifts to broader factors such as demographics and access to rail services (Raymond et al., 2016; Welch et al., 2018). Some of this work does include cross-level interactions whose constituent terms involve both a level-1 and a level-2 variable.

Second Stop: Operationalizing Key Questions

The first three of the cited theoretical questions, but not the fourth, can be operationalized with the current dataset, including the added hypothetical year variable.

(1) Are outcome scores trending significantly upward or significantly downward over the period examined and by how much? In this dataset, as structured, rent can only go up over time. Of course, for many datasets, time's impact could be positive or negative. The specific question becomes whether the average linear impact of year on the outcome is significantly above zero, significantly below zero, or indistinguishable from no change.

(2) Is the annual rate of rent changes speeding up or slowing down over time? Alternatively, is the rate of change constant for the entire period? If the rent change rate does *not* remain constant over the entire period, model predictions will better fit the data if they include, in addition to the predictor capturing the linear impact of time, a second predictor capturing the curvilinear impact of time. A curvilinear component for the impact of time, should it prove significant, also can reveal whether the rate of annual rent increases was speeding up or slowing down in later as compared to earlier portions of the timeframe.

(3) Are annual rates at which rents increase different in different places? Here, do model predictions better fit the data when each property has its own pathway through time (Raudenbush, 2005)? More specifically, does an RCR model allowing varying impacts of linear time at level 2, the property level, do better than an ANCOVA model with just a fixed, average effect of linear time? As in the last chapter, the familiar `lrtest`, along with examinations of BIC and AIC differences, help answer the question.

(4) The fourth question posed previously cannot be answered here. Because there are no separate indicators of property-level attributes, a cross-level interaction with time at level 1 and a property variable at level 2, cannot be built.

If applicable level-2 attribute data were available, however, here is how one would proceed to work towards testing a cross-level interaction. One would decide, using theory, the level-2 attribute that likely moderates the impact of the linear time variable. Then, one would formulate the relevant cross-level interaction term involving the level-1 linear time variable and the specified level-2 attribute. BIC or AIC differences would indicate if adding such a cross-level interaction improves how well model predictions fit the data.

Although current dataset limitations preclude addressing this fourth question, the sequence of models and the model comparisons reviewed here indicate whether formulating a specific cross-level interaction would make sense empirically. If the impacts of time on the outcome variable do not vary significantly across level-2 units, there would be no justification for exploring a cross-level interaction in the first place. In that instance, with one average predicted linear time impact similarly shaping rent changes for all level-2 units, an ANCOVA model would be sufficient. Only if the RCR model were needed would one then try to test a cross-level interaction.

For questions 1 through 3, note two points. The different time questions are independent in that the answer to each relies on an independent statistical test. Nevertheless, the settings of one model parameter may affect the value of other model parameters, or may affect a significance test. A specific answer may be conditioned on how other model parameters are set. As will be shown, this turns out to be an important matter.

Building the Hypothetical Year Variable

Up until now, all the variables included appear on the property deeds themselves, or were generated from analyses of those data. To assist examining rent changes over time, and possible property-level differences in rates of rent change, however, I have added a home-brewed variable to the Monopoly dataset. More precisely, I attached a specific hypothetical year, anywhere from 1880 to 1930, to each specific property at each stage of development. The year indicates the date the specified property attained the specified stage of real estate development. Five rules shaped variable construction.

First, each property has gone through the same sequence of development over time, the same sequence each Monopoly player goes through to develop the properties of a color scheme. Each property starts with bare ground in 1880; renters on that streetblock of the named property bring their own platform tents.[2] Then, one guesthouse goes up, then another, then another, then another, with at least one year between appearances of additional guesthouses. After four guesthouses line the street, the next stage of development, after at least another year has passed, is flattening the guesthouses and putting up a hotel. Imagine a multigenerational family vacationing in the same block on the same street year after year, decade after decade. Different members of the family would see these changes. No reversals in development are allowed.[3]

Second, the time variable baked in the idea that some parts of Atlantic City started developing sooner. Historic maps of Atlantic City from late in the 19th century or early in the 20th century show that the less centrally located properties, further from the intense entertainment zone of the central Boardwalk or further inland, started developing later.[4]

Third, and amplifying the previous point, the development process, once started, proceeded more quickly in more desirable locations, and more slowly in less desirable locations. As mentioned in the last chapter, there is no independent indicator of neighborhood desirability. Instead, the sequence of properties as one progresses around the playing board is used as a proxy for the increasing desirability of location and, therefore, for the speed of real estate development.

In short, the time variable in the data, year, labeled "Hypothetical year," builds in both spatial and temporal variations in real estate development pressures. Values also include a small random component for every development stage for every property.[5]

Fourth, a property *need not* experience *any* real estate transition in a year, or in a stretch of years. A property could remain undeveloped, or remain at any level in the development sequence, for several years. In other words, any property, at any time, could "stall" in the development sequence. Given the spatiotemporal assumption mentioned previously, slower development, or stalled development for a time, was more likely in lower SES locations.

Fifth, all properties must have been fully developed no later than 1930. That is, all properties must have a hotel by or before 1930. The underpinning historical idea here is that by the end of the "Roaring Twenties," enough people from different social strata were vacationing in Atlantic City to create demand for a hotel on every named street, although obviously not every named block. "By 1925 Atlantic City had: more than 1,200 hotels and boardinghouses capable of accommodating nearly 400,000 visitors at a time" (Johnson, 2009, p. 90).

The Hypothetical Year Variable: Two Examples

Perhaps two examples will help clarify how the hypothetical year variable shapes development.

Figure 9.1 shows a graph of rent over time by hypothetical year for Park Place. Of course, each rent increase accompanies each additional level of real estate development. This property developed quickly, which is no surprise, given its proximity to the central portion of the Boardwalk. Starting out undeveloped like all the other properties in 1880, it had one guesthouse after two years, two after six, three after eight, four after nine, and a hotel after twelve, by 1892. The solid line shows a linear trend line for changes in rent, for just this property. Rents rose from $35 in 1880 to $1,500 in 1892, creating annual rent increases of $122.08. The dashed line shows the curvilinear or quadratic impact of each succeeding year. Because the linear and quadratic lines are quite close together, this property's *rate* of yearly development-linked rent increases was not faster in earlier as compared to later years; nor was it faster in later as compared to earlier years. For Park Place, throughout the period of its development, 1880 through 1892, the rate of rent increase was constant according to this arbitrarily constructed time variable.

Table 9.1 shows the same data in a table. It also includes, in the middle column, the hypothetical year variable centered on 1900 (c_yr1900). A centered hypothetical year variable, capturing the predicted linear impact of time on rent, is needed because models will also include a variable capturing curvilinear temporal impact. Typically, when a variable is centered, its mean is removed. The mean of year is 1898.55. Here, instead of the mean,

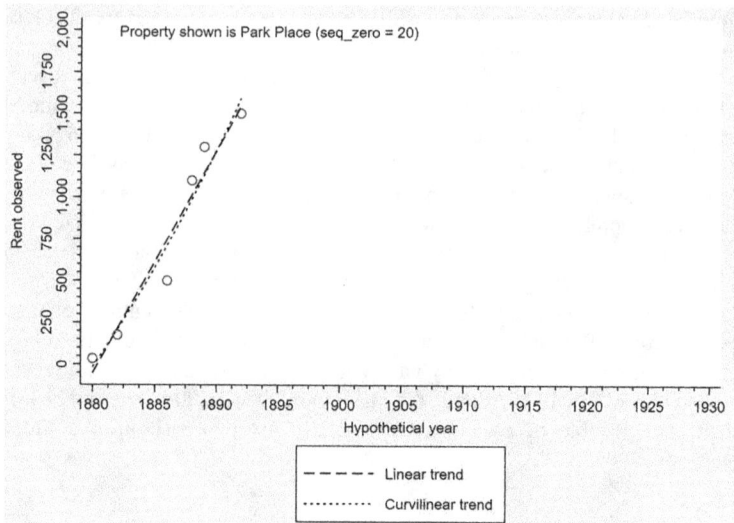

Figure 9.1 Park Place, linear and curvilinear development trends.

Table 9.1 Park Place, levels of development and rent by hypothetical year

Stage of development	Hypothetical year	Hypothetical year variable centered on 1900 (c_yr1900)	Rent
0 guesthouse, no hotel	1880	−20	$35
1 guesthouse, no hotel	1882	−18	$175
2 guesthouses, no hotel	1886	−14	$500
3 guesthouses, no hotel	1888	−12	$1,100
4 guesthouses, no hotel	1889	−11	$1,300
0 guesthouse, 1 hotel	1892	−8	$1,500

Note: Property = Park Place (seq_zero = 20). Centered variable subtracts 1900 from hypothetical year variable

the value of 1900 is removed.[6] This makes interpreting model intercepts more straightforward.

Oriental Avenue paints a contrasting picture. Development-linked rent increases were much slower overall. See Figure 9.2, with property-specific linear and curvilinear predicted time trends superimposed on rent data. Note the comparative differences. (1) The predicted linear rate of growth is much slower on Oriental Avenue than on Park Place. The hotel appears much later

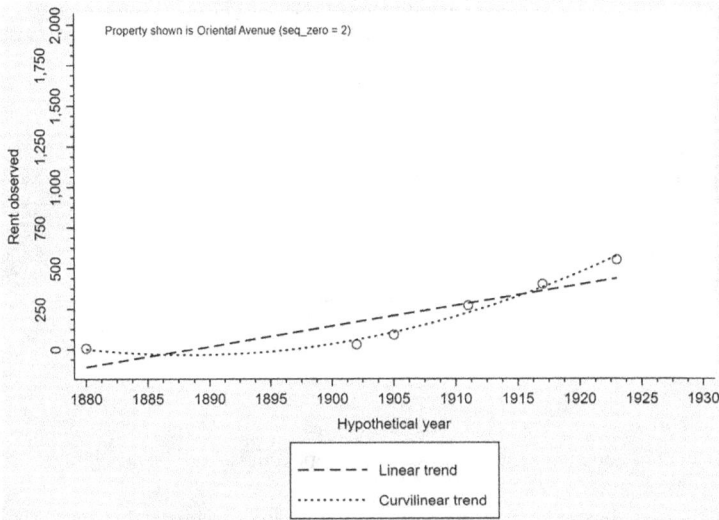

Figure 9.2 Oriental Avenue, linear and curvilinear development trends.

on Oriental Avenue than on Park Place: 1923 rather than 1892. (2) Further, once fully developed, rents on Oriental are much lower than on Park Place. (3) Moreover, the separation between the line showing the predicted linear time trend, and the curve indicating predicted curvilinear time trend, suggests fluctuation in the rate of rent increases. Development sped up in later years after a slow initial phase. This contrasts with the largely consistent linear rate of rent increases on Park Place.

Table 9.2 shows the development data for Oriental Avenue. The first guesthouse did not appear until 22 years into the period (1902). The pace of development picked up somewhat thereafter. A second guesthouse appeared three years later (1905). An additional guesthouse appeared six years later (1911), and another one six years after that (1917). The property was fully developed, with a hotel, by 1923. On average over the period, rents increased yearly by $12.65.

Operationalizing Linear and Curvilinear Temporal Components

Linear Time Impact Variable

As already noted, the linear time variable used in the model (c_yr1900) was centered on 1900. There were two reasons. First, 1900 is very close to the mean of the time variable, 1898.55. With centering on 1900, interpreting the

Table 9.2 Oriental Avenue, levels of development and rent by hypothetical year

Stage of development	Hypothetical year	Hypothetical year variable centered on 1900 (c_yr1900)	Rent
0 guesthouse, no hotel	1880	−20	$6
1 guesthouse, no hotel	1902	2	$30
2 guesthouses, no hotel	1905	5	$90
3 guesthouses, no hotel	1911	11	$270
4 guesthouses, no hotel	1917	17	$400
0 guesthouse, 1 hotel	1923	23	$550

Note: Property = Oriental Avenue (seq_zero = 2). Centered variable subtracts 1900 from hypothetical year variable.

constant in equations with a linear time component is easy: "The average rent was X dollars in 1900."

Second, beyond rendering the constant readily interpretable, centering permits creating linear and curvilinear time variables which are not collinear (Aiken & West, 1991).[7] The curvilinear time variable (yrsq1900) is created by squaring the centered linear time variable. Without centering, the two time variables would correlate too strongly.

Curvilinear Time Impact

The quadratic or curvilinear time variable (yrsq1900), created by squaring the centered year variable, allows learning whether development sped up or slowed down later in the period as compared to earlier.[8] With this setup, the correlation between the two temporal component variables is weak, $r = .07$.[9]

A Confession

Recall that deciding whether a multilevel model is needed involves looking for a significant LR χ^2 value with the ANOVA model. The alert reader will see that when the data are clustered by individual property, *this value is nonsignificant, and therefore multilevel models are not needed*:

```
LR test vs. linear model:chibar2(01) = 0.97 Prob >=
chibar2=0.1619
```

That is absolutely the correct conclusion. Nevertheless, the guideline is ignored here, given this chapter's pedagogical purposes: illustrating the fundamentals when applying multilevel models to longitudinal data.

Third Stop: Model Selection

Just a quick reminder about the different data structure in this chapter. The level-2 unit is the individual property deed. Different neighborhoods are ignored. As before, the level-1 unit of observation is rent value for a particular property at a particular stage of property development. Now, however, each rent value also has a year attached to it.

Run the following model sequence:

1. ANOVA or null model.
2. ANCOVA model with (i) average impact of linear time.
3. ANCOVA model with (i) average impact of linear time and (ii) average impact of curvilinear time.
4. RCR capturing up to three impacts of time: (i) average impact of linear time; (ii) average impact of curvilinear time; *and* (iii) a random effect for linear time, allowing different *b* weights for predicted impacts of linear time on rent, for each different property. The latter allows each property to have its own linear time trend predicting rent changes. With this option, each property charts its own pathway of rent changes through time (Raudenbush, 2005).
5. Assess AIC and BIC for each model in the sequence (*2* vs. *3*; then *4* vs. *3* or *2*). Use this as a preliminary decision guide to decide which model is best. The LR χ^2 also can help gauge the significance of improvements in how well model predictions fit data.
6. Test for serial autocorrelation. Reassess the model after considering serial autocorrelation.

Background on Step 6: Serial Autocorrelation

Step 6 is not feasible with these data. This is simply another limitation of working with this dataset.[10] Nonetheless, a basic understanding of serial autocorrelation is required if applying multilevel models to longitudinal data. Here are some of the basics. For more details, see Twisk (2013, pp. 107–117).[11]

With a longitudinal data series, the autocorrelation problem arises from serial or temporal autocorrelation. That is, for a level-2 unit, later outcome scores may be influenced by earlier outcome scores. Such dependencies violate model assumptions and demand consideration in model specification.

Here, Parker Brothers game designers made it so that each property's rents at later stages of real estate development depend in part on rents at earlier stages. More specifically, when stages of real estate development are organized longitudinally and at the property level, as is done in this chapter, these data have an autoregressive structure. Ideally, the models used would account for that non-independence or serial autocorrelation. This situation violates the regression assumption of independent residuals.

In the simplest terms, an autoregressive structure exists here because when predicting rent for a particular property (*P*) at stage of development (*d*), that rent value will be strongly correlated with the rent value for property *P* at the previous stage of development, *d* - 1. More technically:

> the correlations one measurement apart [in time] are assumed to be [correlated with a strength of] ρ [rho]; correlations two measurements apart are assumed to be [correlated with a strength of] ρ^2; correlations *t* measurements apart are assumed to be [correlated with a strength of] ρ^t.
>
> (Twisk, 2013, p. 58)

Such a structure results in temporally adjacent residuals correlating significantly with one another. One handles this by telling the model to expect residuals with an autoregressive structure. More specifically, models typically start by specifying

> a "first-order" autoregressive model, because the outcome variable *Y* at time point *t* is only related to the value of the outcome variable *Y* at *t*−1 . . . the idea underlying the [first-order] autoregressive model is that the value of an outcome variable at each time-point is primarily influenced by the value of this variable one measurement earlier.
>
> (Twisk, 2013, p. 108)

In essence, this allows each property's rent residual at time *t* to correlate with its rent residual at time *t* − 1. Out in the real world, at least in the US and at the level of metropolitan areas, commercial real estate rent growth rates indeed do have a first-order autoregressive structure (Plazzi et al., 2010).

Model specification then typically proceeds by examining whether, in addition to this significant first-order autoregressive structure, "the outcome variable *Y* at time point *t* is also related to the value of the outcome variable *Y* at *t*−2 [a second-order autoregressive structure] or *t*−3 [a third-order autoregressive structure]" (Twisk, 2013, p. 108).

Comparing Results Across the Model Sequence

Turning back to what is feasible with these data, results shown in Table 9.3 answer the following questions: for each of the three indicators – the LR χ^2 test, changes in AIC, and changes in BIC – how well do model predictions fit observed data? Do models later in the sequence perform better?

Both the AIC and BIC differences suggest improvement at each stage in the sequence. Differences are always greater than −2 (Long, 1997, p. 112), with AIC and BIC values decreasing for models later in the sequence. The LR χ^2 tests, similarly, suggest Model 2 is better than Model 1, 3 is better than 2, and 4 is better than 3. Therefore, at least until we start looking under the hood,

Table 9.3 Comparing models: information criterion statistic differences, and likelihood ratio χ^2 test results

Model sequence	Model 1 (ANOVA)	Model 2 (ANCOVA with average (i.e., fixed) effect for linear time)	Model 3 (ANCOVA with average effects for both linear time and curvilinear time)	Model 4 (RCR with average effects for both linear time and curvilinear time, and varying (i.e., random) effects for linear time)
1 LR χ^2 test, ΔAIC, and ΔBIC are comparing:		Model 2 versus Model 1	Model 3 versus Model 2	Model 4 versus Model 3
2 LR χ^2 test		$\chi^2(df = 1) = 54.33; p < .0005$	$\chi^2(df = 1) = 7.55; p < .005$	$\chi^2(df = 2) = 140.30; p < .0005$
3 AIC	1,992.47	1,940.15	1,934.60	1,798.31
4 BIC	2,001.12	1,951.68	1,949.02	1,818.49
5 ΔAIC		52.32	5.55	136.29
6 ΔBIC		49.44	2.66	130.53

Note: Δ = change. Model names align with columns in Table 9.5. LR = likelihood ratio. AIC = Akaike Information Criterion information measure. BIC = Bayes Information Criterion information measure. As recommended, naïve p-values for the LR χ^2 tests have been divided by two (Rabe-Hesketh & Skrondal, 2012a: 198).

Model 4 appears to be the preferred model, with its predictions doing the best in fitting the observed data. The command line generating this model is:

```
mixed rent c_yr1900 yrsq1900 || seq_zero: c_yr1900
```

Note three time components allowed:

- An average predicted linear impact of year after removing 1900 (c_yr1900). Technically, this is a fixed or average linear effect of time on rent.
- An average predicted curvilinear impact of squared time (yrsq1900). Technically, this is a fixed or average quadratic effect of time on rent, operating in addition to the average linear effect of time on rent.
- A rent impact of linear time varying from property to property. It appears at the end of the command line following the colon (:). It allows predicted property-level departures from the average predicted linear rent impact of c_yr1900. Each property now has its own *b* weight for the predicted rent impact of linear time. Using Raudenbush's (2005) terminology, this model allows each property to have its own "pathway [of increasing rents] through time"; *b* weights are EB adjusted, shrinking them toward the average *b* weight.

Fourth Stop: Interpreting the Preferred Model

It is almost time to interpret the results of preferred Model 4.

Interpreting Linear and Quadratic Components of Temporal Impact

Before decoding results, however, some orientation about interpreting linear and curvilinear *b* weights for time in tandem may help. See Table 9.4.

In the Monopoly dataset, ignoring selling back to the bank via mortgaging the property, the predicted linear time impact can never be negative. Development proceeds, rents elevate, and the hypothetical year variable progresses.

In other longitudinal data sources, however, the predicted linear impact of time on an outcome could be positive, negative, or flat. For example, a researcher might be examining crime in a period of declining rates (Parker, 2008).

The interpretation of the direction of the *b* weight for the predicted curvilinear time impact depends on the direction of the predicted linear time impact. Here, in the context of a predicted positive average linear impact of time on rent, a significant predicted curvilinear time impact would signify one of two things. If positive, it would mean rents rose *faster later* in the period. If negative, it would mean rents rose *more slowly later* in the period.

Table 9.4 General guidelines on interpreting linear and quadratic (curvilinear) *b* weights for temporal trends when both included in a model

If the predicted linear temporal trend is:	And the predicted curvilinear departure is:	Then your interpretation is:
Positive	Positive	Outcome scores trended noticeably upward over the entire series; further, they trended upward more sharply (more steeply) toward the end of the series.
Positive	Negative	Outcome scores trended noticeably upward over the series; that upward trend, however, slowed i.e., became flatter or reversed somewhat, toward the end of the series.
Positive	Nonsignificant	Outcome scores trended noticeably upward, and at a relatively constant rate, throughout the entire series.
Negative	Positive	Outcome scores trended noticeably downward over the entire series, but the downward trend became more gradual, i.e., became flatter or reversed somewhat, toward the end of the series.
Negative	Negative	Outcome scores trended noticeably downward over the entire series; that downward trend, however, became more marked, i.e., became steeper, toward the end of the series.
Negative	Nonsignificant	Outcome scores trended noticeably downward, and at a relatively constant rate, throughout the entire series.
Nonsignificant	Positive	Although outcome scores did *not* exhibit an overall upward or downward trend for the entire series, scores trended noticeably downward earlier in the series then noticeably upward later in the series.
Nonsignificant	Negative	Although outcome scores did *not* exhibit an overall upward or downward trend for the entire series, scores trended noticeably upward earlier in the series then noticeably downward later in the series

Note: "Positive" means a positive, statistically significant coefficient. "Negative" means a statistically significant negative coefficient. "Nonsignificant" means a statistically nonsignificant coefficient. Testing of a curvilinear temporal component requires including the corresponding linear temporal component in the same model.

The interpretation of a significant average predicted curvilinear time impact is different if the average predicted linear time impact is negative. In that context, a positive curvilinear impact suggests that the overall downward trend over the period slowed down later in the data series; a negative curvilinear impact suggests that the overall downward trend steepened, or picked up speed, later in the data series.

Finally, a predicted average curvilinear temporal impact can be significant in the context of a nonsignificant predicted average linear temporal impact.

Interpreting Results From the Preferred Model

Preferred Model 4 (Table 9.5) includes three temporal components: (1) the average predicted linear impact of time on rent, (2) the average predicted curvilinear impact of time, and (3) as part of the random or varying effects in the model, property-level deviations from the average linear impact of time. This model's results are interpreted here and occasionally contrasted with results from the previous model in the sequence.

Intercept

See line 9 in Table 9.5. The constant, $744.39, reflects average predicted rent when all predictors scored zero. This corresponds to 1900 given how the two time variables were centered. One can say, "The average predicted rent on a property in 1900 was $744.39." This is just a descriptive statement.

Average Impact of Linear Time

See lines 1–4 in Table 9.5. In Model 4, on average, for each additional hypothetical year, predicted rent increased $45.70. This is an *average* development-driven linear trend of increasing rent over time for all properties. It arose from more than random noise ($t = 5.05$; $p < .001$).

Average Curvilinear Impact of Time: Was the Rate of Change Changing?

Did the average predicted rate of yearly rent increases vary across the period from 1880 to 1930? Model 4 says yes; see lines 5–8, Table 9.5. `yrsq1900` had a predicted, significant, positive impact ($b = .34$; $p < .001$). With a significant positive linear trend, and a significant positive curvilinear trend, predicted year-on-year rent increases were steeper later in the period as compared to earlier (Table 9.4), according to these model results.

Table 9.5 Predicting impacts of time: Null model, linear time, linear+curvilinear, and varying time effects

Model	1	2	3	4
	(ANOVA or null model)	(ANCOVA model with average (i.e., fixed) effect for linear time)	(ANCOVA model with average effects for both linear time and curvilinear time)	(RCR model with average effects for both linear time and curvilinear time, and varying (i.e., random) effects for linear time)
Predictor				
1 Hypothetical year centered on 1900		$22.955	$22.700	$45.700
2 (linear temporal impact)		($2.277)	($2.218)	($9.046)
3		10.081	10.233	5.052
4		p < .001	p < .001	p < .001
5 Hypothetical year centered on 1900 squared				
(curvilinear temporal impact)			-$0.408	$0.344
6			($0.146)	($0.074)
7			-2.788	4.682
8			p < .01	p < .001
9 Intercept/Constant	$469.061	$502.276	$577.030	$744.385
10	($44.496)	($78.943)	($80.265)	($178.239)
Random effects parameters				
11 var(_cons)	$11,767.278	$121,435.690	$110,992.131	$691,953.750
12	($13,814.916)	($43,307.389)	($40,021.145)	($215,475.871)

(Continued)

Table 9.5 (Continued)

Model	1 (ANOVA or null model)	2 (ANCOVA model with average (i.e., fixed) effect for linear time)	3 (ANCOVA model with average effects for both linear time and curvilinear time)	4 (RCR model with average effects for both linear time and curvilinear time, and varying (i.e., random) effects for linear time)
13 var(c_yr1900)				$1,758.553
14				($565.896)
15 cov(c_yr1900_cons)				$34,883.196
16				($11,007.483)
17 var(e)	$190,742.767	$92,579.622	$87,933.506	$17,565.933
18	($25,719.693)	($12,600.855)	($11,984.520)	($2,381.013)
Model parameters				
19 N observations	132	132	132	132
20 Log likelihood	−993.24	−966.07	−962.30	−892.15
21 AIC	1992.47	1940.15	1934.60	1798.31
22 BIC	2001.12	1951.68	1949.02	1818.49
23 Wald χ^2 model test	.	101.64	114.24	45.41
24 Model test p-value		< .001	< .001	< .001
25 N RE parameters	2.00	2.00	2.00	4.00
26 N variances	2.00	2.00	2.00	3.00

Note. Standard errors in parentheses. For predictors, rows show b / (se) / t / p < .
Level 1 = individual rent value (n=132); level 2 = property name (n = 22).
var(c_yr1900) = variance of varying b weights for linear temporal impact.
var(_cons) = level 2 residual variance.
cov(c_yr1900,_cons) = covariance between varying linear time impact and level 2 residuals.
var(e) = level 1 residual variance.

The predicted positive curvilinear impact of time in Model 4, however, causes consternation. In Model 3, the corresponding *b* weight is *negative* ($b = -.41$; $p < .01$). The Model 3 result indicates predicted rent increases slowed down, rather than sped up, for later years in the 1880–1930 period. This contrast is revisited when checking under the hood, at the next stop.

Variations in Predicted Impacts of Linear Time Create a Variance for the Linear Slopes

See lines 13–14 [var(c_yr1900)] in Table 9.5. These report the variance (τ_{11}), and its standard error, for the predicted level-2 slope-deviations-from-average-slope for linear time. This variance is built from EB-adjusted slope deviations around the average predicted rent impact for linear time.

The ratio of the variance $1,758.55, to its standard error, $565.90, provides a one-tailed *z* test ($z = 3.1$; $p < .01$) for the null hypothesis that the variation in these slopes is zero. The variation does appear to be more than mere noise.[12] In short, these results suggest the predicted *yearly rate* of rent increases was higher for some properties compared to others.

Fifth Stop: Checking Under the Hood of the Preferred Model

Some Sensible Results so Far

So far, the preferred model, with two average rent impacts for time and one varying rent impact for time, has produced sensible and interpretable results.

1. The AIC and BIC differences both show Model 4 is an improvement, controlling for complexity, over the previous Model 3 which allows only the two average impacts of time on rent. LR χ^2 test results agree Model 4 with three rent impacts of time is the preferred model.
2. In Model 4, the *b* weights for predicted linear and curvilinear time impacts on rent are both significant, meaning, here, each is unlikely to have arisen solely from random noise in the data.
3. In Model 4, the two coefficients for average time impacts are both positive, meaning that predicted rents went up over time, and did so faster toward the end of the period.
4. In Model 4, when each property carves its own pathway through time for rent increases, those 22 level-2 slope departures from the average predicted rent impact of linear time produce a variance three times its standard error. These varying impacts of linear time are more than random variation.

But Also Some Worries

Despite all the good news, do not fall in love with Model 4 results yet.

Positive or Negative Curvilinear Impact of time?

One concern already has surfaced. The curvilinear impact of time is positive in Model 4, but negative in Model 3. This is an example of "beta bounce" (Gordon, 1968), a coefficient flipping from being significant in one direction to being significant in the opposite direction. Such coefficient flipping is disconcerting and preferably avoided. Often it arises from collinearity among predictors in a model. Steps taken here, however, separated the linear and curvilinear time predictors. Consequently, something is probably going on elsewhere in the model that is causing this flipping.

One approach to checking further on whether the curvilinear impact "should" be positive or negative is to look at the actual data pattern. That pattern is examined shortly.

Inflated Standard Errors in Model 4

A second concern is that some standard errors in Model 4 are multiples of their values in Model 3. Consider, for example, the standard error for the predicted linear impact of time in Models 3 and 4 (Table 9.5, line 2). Standard error inflation is another hint of a multicollinearity concern somewhere in the model (Darlington, 1990, p. 130). Since the predictors are not involved, perhaps other model parameters are playing a role.

In Short

In short, the main takeaway so far, after looking closely at the results in Table 9.5, and considering how some things change from Model 3 to Model 4, is this. Although Model 4 has a lot going for it, and seems the best based on the indicators for model-selection (Table 9.3), the model has worrisome features. One standard error inflates markedly going from Model 3 to Model 4, and one coefficient changes direction.

Generate Predictions and Residuals From Preferred Model

The next step in looking under the hood for Model 4 is to generate predicted scores, and residuals, both at level 1 and level 2. Be careful; there are many options. Examine the Stata mixed postestimation help file for predict.

Residual diagnostic plots of level-1 residuals do not suggest the time RCR model is problematic in obvious ways. For example, Figure 9.3 plots predicted rent values from the model (horizontal axis) against level-1 model

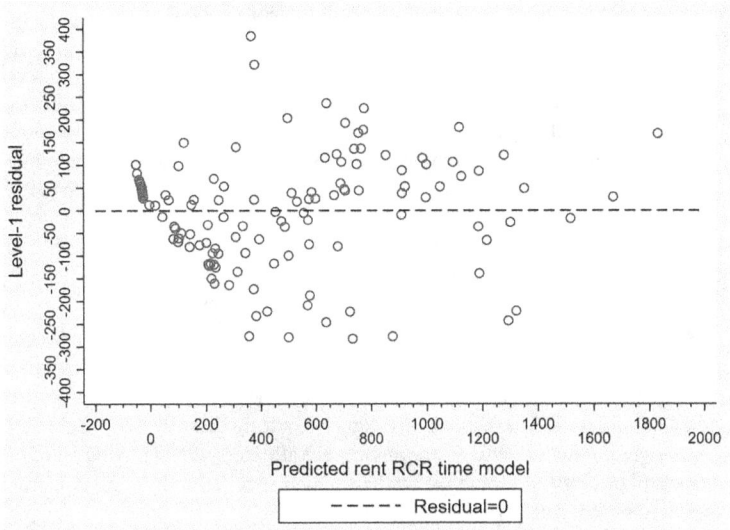

Figure 9.3 Level-1 residuals versus predicted values from longitudinal RCR model of temporal impacts on rent.

residuals (y-axis). Although there are two high residual values somewhat separated from the other values in the scatterplot, residuals, generally, are evenly distributed above and below the reference line of zero.[13]

Inspecting Level-2 Slope and Intercept Residuals

Time to more closely examine level-2 residuals. These include the residuals for the level-2 slope deviations (u_{1j} values) from the average rent impact of the linear time variable, and level-2 rent residuals (u_{0j} values).

Preliminary Considerations

Five preliminary points:

1. In a model with *both* varying slopes for one predictor, *and* varying level-2 residuals from the overall intercept, each is generated in the order in which it appears in the random-effects portion of the output table. Stata will provide a variable label, so *always* check these variables with the describe command to avoid confusion about which is which.
2. Stata attaches these level-2, property-level values to individual records. A collapsed file at level 2 ($n = 22$) will be needed for further investigation.

3. Values are expressed as deviations from the corresponding average value. Add deviations to the respective average values to get EB-estimated property-level slopes for linear time impacts and EB-estimated property-level residuals for the outcome.
4. Given empirical Bayes estimation, expect shrinkage for both level-2 slope deviations and level-2 outcome residuals. Slope deviation shrinkage may be more substantial than intercept residual shrinkage (Raudenbush & Bryk, 2002, pp. 88–89).
5. Stata simultaneously estimates two independent sets of random effects and the correlation or covariance between them. Pay close attention to how tightly bound the two sets of random effects are. "The empirical Bayes estimate of each [random] component will depend on the other component. This dependence will be strong when the maximum likelihood estimate of the correlation between the two components is large" (Raudenbush & Bryk, 2002, p. 89). Again, as in Chapter 8, strong dependency would suggest the two random effects parameters are afflicted with semantic ambiguity (Abbott, 1997), making it unclear which specific underlying construct each indicator reflects.

Doing it

With the `predict` postestimation command, the `reffects` option "calculates best linear unbiased predictions (BLUPs) . . . of the random effects" (Rabe-Hesketh & Skrondal, 2012a, p. 441).

Follow the `predict` command with the `describe` command to show variable labels for each random component. In the `random-effects parameters` section of the online `log` output file for Model 4, *not* Table 9.5, the variance of linear time [`var(c_yr1900)`] appears before the variance of the level-2 residuals [`var(_cons)`]. Therefore, when the residuals are created, `pre_rnt_re1` corresponds to the linear time slope deviations, and `pre_rnt_re2` corresponds to the level-2 outcome residuals.[14]

After the `collapse` operation, the online code adds the average linear time slope to each slope deviation, and the constant to each level-2 intercept residual, to get predicted values, rather than predicted deviations.

Growing Your Way Into the Specific Results for the Time Slopes

First, examine the varying slopes descriptively, and see if they suggest some patterns. See Table 9.6. The 22 properties are sorted from lowest to highest predicted linear rent increases.

The order column (A) indicates property rank, from lowest to highest, based on year-on-year predicted rent changes. Properties where annual rents were increasing faster appear lower in the listing. Column B shows property

Table 9.6 Varying predicted linear impacts of hypothetical year at property level, expressed as estimated slopes and as EB-adjusted deviations from average estimated slope for linear time

Order	Property name	Property deed in sequence going around the board (seq_zero)	Predicted linear yearly increase in rent: model estimate	Predicted linear yearly increase in rent: model estimate expressed as deviation from average linear impact of year
A	B	C	D	E
1	Mediterranean	0	$5.69	−$40.01
2	Vermont	3	$9.35	−$36.35
3	Baltic	1	$9.50	−$36.20
4	Oriental	2	$11.90	−$33.80
5	Connecticut	4	$13.28	−$32.42
6	St. Charles	5	$15.28	−$30.42
7	States	6	$16.38	−$29.32
8	Virginia	7	$19.78	−$25.92
9	St. James	8	$24.45	−$21.25
10	Tennessee	9	$26.69	−$19.01
11	Kentucky	11	$31.59	−$14.11
12	Indiana	12	$31.91	−$13.79
13	Illinois	13	$34.99	−$10.71
14	New York	10	$39.08	−$6.62
15	Ventnor	15	$48.71	$3.01
16	Atlantic	14	$49.59	$3.89
17	Marvin Gardens	16	$64.87	$19.17
18	No. Carolina	18	$71.66	$25.96
19	Pacific	17	$77.65	$31.95
20	Pennsylvania	19	$96.50	$50.80
21	Park Place	20	$140.04	$94.34
22	Boardwalk	21	$166.52	$120.82

Note: Results from longitudinal random coefficients regression (RCR) model predicting rent (Table 9.5, Model 4, with year centered on 1900). Properties sorted from lowest to highest estimated linear impact of hypothetical year on rent. Column C shows order in the sequence of properties as one progresses around the board. Column D shows the estimated linear impact of hypothetical year. Column E shows deviation from estimated average linear impact of hypothetical year. Hypothetical year is an author-constructed variable, with values ranging from 1880–1928, assigning each stage of real estate development of each property to a particular hypothetical year.

names. Column C references where each property appeared in the sequence of properties going around the board. This is the level-2 organizing variable, seq_zero. Column D reports property-specific slopes for predicted annual rent increases. Column E shows the same information, but now each property's predicted annual rent increase is expressed as a deviation from the average predicted annual rent increase.[15]

To dig deeper, consider Park Place. Rents increased from $35 to $1,500 between 1880 and 1892, for an observed yearly rent increase of $122.08 over the 12-year span. Model 4's EB adjusted estimate of Park Place's predicted annual linear increase in rent ($u_{1,20}$) was $94.34 higher than the average annual increase across all properties. Putting Park Place's higher-than-average predicted annual rent increase ($94.34) together with the overall annual predicted yearly linear rent increase for all properties ($45.70, Table 9.5, Model 4), which is the same as the average slope for linear time (γ_{10}), yields an estimated annual rent increase for Park Place of $140.04 ($b_{1,20}$). This estimate is above the observed rate of annual rent increases.

Oriental Avenue provides another illustration. Rent increased from $6 in 1880 to $550 in 1923, for an average observed annual rent increase of $12.65. Model 4 estimates that Oriental's predicted yearly annual linear rent increase was $33.80 lower ($u_{1,2}$) than the overall predicted annual linear rent increase (γ_{10}) of $45.70 for all properties. Putting the EB-adjusted slope deviation for linear time rent impact together with the average slope yields an estimated annual rent increase ($b_{1,2}$) of $11.90 for this property. This estimate is slightly below the rate of observed annual rent increases.

Checking on the Correlation Between the Two Random Parameters

Time to examine the correlation between the level-2 rent residuals (u_{0j}) and the level-2 slope departures from the average predicted linear impact of c_yr1900 (u_{1j}). Running the mixed command with the stddeviations option for Model 4, or constructing a scatterplot of the two parameters, reveals the same answer. These two varying parameters in the model in effect correlate perfectly with each other, making them completely collinear with one another. That collinearity renders the results of RCR Model 4 suspect and helps explain some of the oddities observed with beta bounce and inflating standard errors.

What to Conclude About the Preferred Model After All the Checking Under the Hood?

The RCR model, despite the decision-making tools used for model selection pointing favorably toward it (Table 9.3), and despite many seemingly sensible results, should not be trusted.[16] With these Monopoly data, it is not possible to chart each property's individual "pathway [of rent increases] through time."

What is seen here is analogous to what we witnessed in Chapter 8. There, we saw an extremely powerful correlation between varying hotel rent impacts and level-2, neighborhood-level residuals. Here, level-2 slope deviations, making the predicted rent impacts of linear time stronger or weaker for different properties, could not be separated from property-level rent residuals.

Therefore, here, as in Chapter 8, semantic ambiguity ensues. Here, each of the two random effects indicators in this analysis cannot be clearly tied to its corresponding underlying theoretical construct. Remember: this is not just about stats; it is about stats and theory.

Sixth Stop: If All Else Fails, Look at the Data, Then Revisit Preferred Model Decision

The most salient discrepancy between ANCOVA and RCR results is the "beta bounce" observed for the impact of curvilinear time. Did the rate of annual rent increases slow down later in the time frame (Table 9.5, Model 3) or speed up (Table 9.5, Model 4)? Inspection of a graph may help sort this matter out. What do the actual data reveal about this expected curvilinear relationship? See Figure 9.4.

Hypothetical year appears on the horizontal axis, and observed rent on the vertical axis. The circles are just data, not model results. Circle size increases with neighborhood SES, increasing in size as one turns each corner of the playing board.

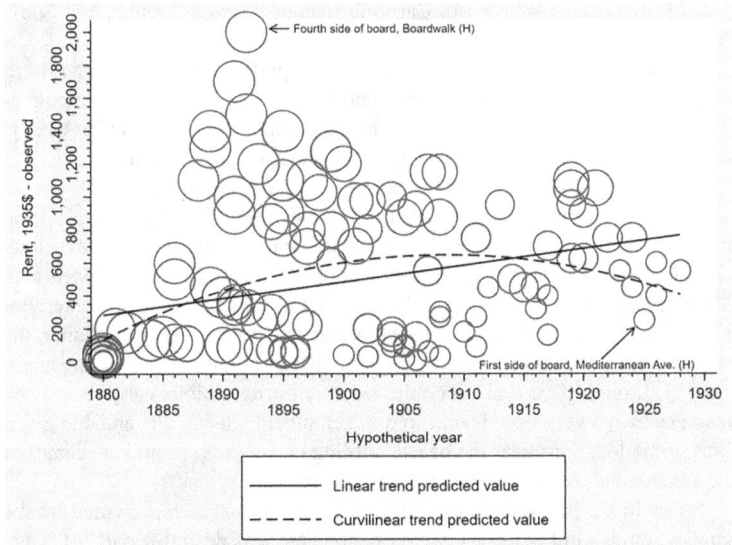

Figure 9.4 Observed rent plotted against hypothetical year, with linear and curvilinear trend lines based on observed data shown. Larger circles correspond to higher SES neighborhoods.

The graph includes two trends, one linear, one curvilinear. These trends are not multilevel model results, just trends fitted to the data. They are fitted to the data points using the Stata graph functions lfit for a linear fit, the solid line, and qfit for a quadratic fit, the dashed line.

Note the dashed curvilinear trend is *negative*. Since it curves downward, it indicates the rate of yearly rent increases slowed later in the period. The negative fitted curvilinear trend seen here aligns with the negative *b* weight reported by Model 3 in Table 9.5 showing a predicted negative curvilinear impact of year^2 on the rate of rent increases.

Consequently, this trend-fitting examination suggests that the results from the ANCOVA multilevel model (Model 3, Table 9.5) with just two time components, an average linear impact for year (c_yr1900) and an average curvilinear impact for year^2 (c_yrsq1900), align better with the scatterplotted data. That model generates an estimated positive average linear time impact and an estimated *negative* average curvilinear time impact. Both patterns are visible in Figure 9.4.

Would a negative curvilinear trend for year^2 make sense given the context of Atlantic City in the late 1800s and early 1900s? A case can be made that it does. The largest circles in Figure 9.4 are for properties from Pacific Avenue to the Boardwalk, on the fourth side of the playing board. All of these properties on this side include avenues that are either at the ocean beach, like Boardwalk and Park Place, or no more than a few hundred feet from the ocean beach, like South North Carolina Avenue, Pacific Avenue, and South Pennsylvania Avenue.

The hypothetical year variable has these properties rapidly hurtling toward hotel development status in the 1880s and 1890s. That feature of the hypothetical year variable aligns with what was happening on the ground in Atlantic City during these periods, as revealed by historical aero view maps.

We already have seen the 1911 aero view (Figure 2.1). Atlantic City aero-views also are available for 1880,[17] 1900,[18] and 1905.[19] The 1880 versus 1900 contrast in aero views for this section of the city proves particularly revealing. The blocks closest to the ocean beach start out relatively undeveloped and, 20 years later, end up thickly populated with hotels, while extensive entertainment piers appear and jut out into the ocean. In a corresponding manner, the hypothetical year variable has the highest SES locations on the playing board moving through their real estate development progressions early, becoming very expensive very fast. Their rapid development was understandable given their prime locations near the beach, cooling ocean breezes, and the center of the amusement district.

By contrast, properties on the first side of the board, represented by the smallest circles in Figure 9.4, were on streets in less desirable parts of town, further away from both the ocean beach and the most notable entertainment amenities. The hypothetical year variable has these properties developing more slowly over time. The slower progression through the six stages of real estate development, combined with lower overall rents, creates lower rates of annual rent increases.

The slower-paced real estate development for these properties on the fourth side of the board captured with the hypothetical year variable aligns with what historical aero-view maps show. For example, look at Baltic and Mediterranean Avenues in the 1900 aero-view,[20] or as previously pointed out, consider Mediterranean Avenue circa 1911 (Figure 2.1). On many blocks of these named streets, there was not much development for a long period.

Stated differently, according to the values in the hypothetical year variable, in the *later* years of the period, the cheaper properties on the first side(s) of the board continued to develop. This was in contrast to the more expensive properties on the fourth side of the board that had developed to the hotel stage in the *earlier* years in the period. In short, the most expensive rent *increases* associated with real estate development occurred during the early years of the 1880–1930 period, and the least expensive development-linked increases occurred in the later years of the period.

Thus, the negative curvilinear trend, indicating rates of annual rent increases slowing later in the period, makes some sense. That trend appears (1) in this plot here (Figure 9.4) and (2) in the results for ANCOVA Model 3 (Table 9.5). Further, the slowing rate of annual rent increases later in the period (3) aligns with geographically disparate development patterns evident in a historical aero view series. All these points speaks in favor of selecting ANCOVA Model 3 as the preferred model.

Seventh Stop: Reflection

Choosing Models

One last thought on model selection. Generally, it is wisest to select a model that (1) passes inspection after looking under the hood at key model details and key model comparisons, and (2) makes better sense in light of observed data patterns. The latter is especially important when working in the policy world and/or on applied problems. When sharing model results and their implications with non-academics like policymakers or other stakeholders, cross-referencing model results with visible data patterns helps listeners more readily grasp implications of results and, perhaps, increases their willingness to trust model results.

Different Model Results Can Carry Markedly Different Implications in Real-World Contexts

Always take modeling decisions seriously. Yes, we are just playing with Monopoly data here and, in this chapter, with a hypothetical time variable to boot. Nonetheless, even in this situation, model choice has two broad implications, one theoretical, one historical. Does each property get its own "pathway through time" for rent increases or not? Did rent increases speed up or slow down later in the time frame considered?

Sometimes, the modeling decision of whether each place gets its own pathway through time can carry important policy implications. Consider two studies examining shifts in support over time for welfare spending across different regions in Germany. These investigations consider whether that support is influenced by the proportion of immigrants in each region. The dataset used, like the one here, had observations at multiple time points.

The first study found that higher proportions of immigrants in a region significantly reduced support for welfare spending. "Our results suggest that native-born populations become more reluctant to support welfare programs when the proportion of foreigners at the regional level increases" (Schmidt-Catran & Spies, 2016, abstract). That initial study, however, did not allow different attitude shift pathways through time for different parts of the country.

In a later study, Auspurg et al. (2019), reanalyzing these data, treated time differently. These researchers allowed regions within Eastern Germany and Western Germany to follow "heterogeneous trends" (p. 759) over time for changes in support of welfare spending. "Time trends [in support for social welfare] strongly differed between Western and Eastern Germany after reunification" (abstract). Auspurg and colleagues consider these different trends by "adding interaction terms between the year dummies and the [former] East [Germany] dummy" (p. 759). After adding these cross-level interaction terms, with year dummy variables at level 1 and the East Germany dummy variable at level 2, Auspurg and colleagues (2019) found a markedly different result with significantly different policy implications. "We find no evidence that increasing proportions of foreigners undermine welfare support" (abstract).

In short, when working with real longitudinal data, how time is modeled can significantly shape answers to substantive questions.

Pathways Through Time and Moving Toward Theorizing and Testing Cross-level Interactions

Consider this thought experiment. Suppose it had been possible to produce trustworthy RCR estimates here that matched observed data patterns and whose model parameters were not problematically collinear. Could you formulate a spatiotemporal interaction, expecting the linear rate of yearly rent increases to be more positive, i.e., the rate of annual rent increases to go up faster, for properties on the fourth side of the board? These would include Boardwalk, Park Place, South North Carolina Avenue, Pacific Avenue, and South Pennsylvania Avenue. Blocks on these streets are no more than a few hundred feet from the beach and the ocean.

Here would be one way to proceed. You could construct an oceanfront proximity dummy variable for these properties and interact it with the linear time variable centered on 1900. The resulting cross-level interaction would involve a level-1 variable, `year`, and a level-2 variable, a dummy variable distinguishing the group of properties closest to the most popular segments of oceanfront. The cross-level hypothesis is that predicted annual rates of increasing rent were higher for the properties in proximity to desirable oceanfront.

The underlying real estate economics rationale is as discussed previously. The guesthouse and hotel rental market strengthened fastest in locations within easy walking distance of the most popular sections of oceanfront.

Closing Comments on Rent Change Models

This chapter applied the random coefficient model (RCR) to a temporal rather than a spatial question, using an expanded Monopoly dataset that added a hypothetical year variable to each level of development for each property deed. The outcome focus shifted to the rate of rent increases over time. With individual rents at level 1, and properties at level 2, models examined the overall rate of yearly rent increases, whether those increases sped up or slowed down later in the hypothetical period, and whether each property's pattern of rent changes required its own pathway through time. Standard model selection metrics like BIC preferred the model with heterogeneous time trends, that is, the RCR model allowing varying impacts of linear time across properties. Nevertheless, serious questions arose about the RCR model. (1) Two model parameters are indistinguishable, creating a semantic ambiguity problem. (2) Further, the direction of the predicted curvilinear impact of time on rent was reversed in this model. Close inspection of dataset patterns, and a series of historical images, supported results from the ANCOVA model over the RCR model. That inspection clarified the dynamics behind the negative curvilinear time trend for rent changes.

On the one hand, this is a frustrating turn of events. Once again, the limitations of this dataset create a modeling hurdle.

On the other hand, the turn of events illustrates essential lessons. (1) Insights are gained when closely comparing results across models of increasing complexity. (2) Careful model selection using standardized decision-making tools, albeit helpful most of the time, also can get it wrong. (3) Get under the hood and look at model estimates to reveal crucial details. (4) When revisiting the question of which model is preferred, going back to basic observed data patterns, if available, can be beneficial.

As in so many matters, it is about the process, not the results; the journey, not the destination. The steps outlined in this investigative journey are exactly those to follow for any longitudinal dataset analyzed with multilevel models.

Next Steps in Longitudinal Investigation

As mentioned earlier, a vast array of longitudinal modeling approaches are available to you within Stata. Here are some thoughts on next steps for those wanting to look harder at longitudinal data with multilevel models.

First, get clear on the basics. If the next steps include working extensively with cross-section panel data, numerous extremely helpful texts can assist (Baum, 2006; Cameron & Trivedi, 2010; Twisk, 2013). Stata programs like `xtreg`, `xtgee`, or `xtnbreg` for count models are good places to start.

Of course, some of these models, in some modes, like `xtreg` or `xtnbreg` with fixed effects, have their limitations (Allison & Waterman, 2002). Coming to terms with such limitations is also a key part of the learning process.

Then, once fully familiar with the intricacies of modeling cross-section panel data, proceed to growth-curve modeling (Chou et al., 1998; Duncan et al., 1999), group-based trajectory modeling (Nagin, 2005; Weisburd et al., 2012), or finite-mixture modeling (Masyn, 2013). Again, learn about the flaws (Skardhamar, 2010) as well as the strengths of these analytics.

Keep Basic Concerns Uppermost

It is easy to get lost in longitudinal intricacies, even when working with simple models and simple datasets. Most importantly, be sure you understand the essentials. (1) How is each parameter in the model operating statistically? (2) What does each parameter estimate mean theoretically? (3) How are different model parameter estimates linked to one another? (4) Do those connections cloud our understanding of indicator-construct relationships? (5) Compare across candidate models, examining how introducing or deleting different model parameters affects parameter estimates, including their standard errors. (6) Examine how model estimates align or fail to align with observable patterns in the data analyzed. With these concerns uppermost, it should be feasible to chart a course toward theoretically aligned, theory expanding, and analytically sound model results.

Notes

1 The data structure used here is different in important ways from a cross-section panel data structure. Such a structure has two underlying components. First is "cross section data, where, at a given point in time, units are selected at random from the population" (Wooldridge, 2002, p. 5). The second element is a "panel data (or longitudinal data) [structure] which consist of repeated observations on the same cross section of, say, individuals, households, firms, or cities, over time" (Wooldridge, 2002, p. 6).

One panel design element, however, does not exactly fit here. "Panel data are usually observed at regular time intervals" (Cameron & Trivedi, 2010, p. 236). That is not the case here. Rather, the data structure here simply notes the year each property transitions to the next stage in real estate development.

The data structure here is probably best viewed as analogous to those structures analyzed in "longitudinal studies . . . in psychology [that] identify the timing of onset of new abilities" (Raudenbush, 2001, pp. 501–502). Of interest here is not the onset of new abilities but rather the onset of a later stage of real estate development for each specific property.

2 For summer seaside camp adventures complete with platform tents, circa World War I, albeit not in Atlantic City, see Winfield (1919).

3 Monopoly, according to rulebook 00009-I-Rev 4, allows "Selling properties . . . houses and hotels may be sold back to the Bank at any time for *one-half* the price paid for them" (italics in original). I have ignored this option throughout this volume and continue to do so here.

4 For the 1880 map see: Library of Congress digital ID: www.loc.gov/resource/g3814a.pm005041/

For the 1900 map see: Library of Congress digital ID: www.loc.gov/resource/g3814a.pm005050/

For the 1905 map see: Library of Congress digital ID: www.loc.gov/resource/g3814a.pm005060/

5 See the online Chapter 9 `do` file for specific code.

6 `c_yr1900 = year - 1900`

7 The curvilinear time variable here includes one bend, so it captures the quadratic nonlinear impact of time if the linear impact of time is simultaneously included. A curvilinear variable, of course, could include more than one bend and involve higher-order polynomials of the centered time variable. For simplicity's sake here, the quadratic impact is referenced as a curvilinear impact.

8 `yrsq1900 = (year - 1900) * (year - 1900)`

9 More details appear in the online `log` file.

10 The `do` file for this chapter in the online appendix includes code, below the exit command, to run either `mixed` or `xtreg` models incorporating first-order serial autocorrelation. With the multilevel models, variance estimates for the property-level means, and for the within-property residuals, produce odd results. Some variance estimates increase at least an order of magnitude, while some other estimates go to zero. Such results should not be trusted. This is a problem that can crop up when modeling serial autocorrelation with dynamic panel data (Baum, 2006, pp. 232–233).

Only the `xtreg` fixed-effects models appear to generate sensible results and provide a sensible estimate of rho.

You need not worry about all the technical reasons this happens until you take courses that are more advanced in this area. You are not going to see the serial autocorrelation taken into account with the models shown in this chapter, even though it is sizable and the data have a first-order autoregressive structure as they are configured in this chapter.

11 Concerns linked with spatial autocorrelation are completely ignored in this volume. Nonetheless, just a couple quick thoughts on the matter. When level-2 units are spatial, analyses of cross-sectional data may be bedeviled by problems arising from spatially autocorrelated outcomes (Anselin, 1988, 1995; Baller et al., 2001). With such outcomes, observations nearer one another are more similar (Belotti et al., 2017; Chaix et al., 2005; Cliff & Ord, 1970; Kondo, 2016; Townsley, 2009). Stata SP modules spregress, `spivregress`, and `spxtregress` fit spatial autoregressive models. I am not aware, in Stata v. 17, of any modules for mixed effects spatial autoregressive modules. `spxtregress` handles cross-section panel data, as defined earlier in the chapter.

12 It is a one-tailed rather than a two-tailed z test because the variance can only be equal to or greater than zero.

13 The two highest residuals are Illinois Avenue with three houses ($384) and Indiana Avenue with three houses ($322).

14 The following command generates the residuals:

```
predict pre_rnt_re*, reffects
```

A follow-up describe command provides the needed information:

```
pre_rnt_re1 float %9.0g BLUP r.e. for seq_zero: c_yr1900
pre_rnt_re2 float %9.0g BLUP r.e. for seq_zero: _cons
```

15 In the online do file, this variable, originally pre_rnt_re1, is renamed to time_slope_deviation_seq_zero.

16 The RCR model is still problematic even without the curvilinear impacts of year^2. Results not shown.

17 Library of Congress digital ID: www.loc.gov/resource/g3814a.pm005041/

18 Library of Congress digital ID: www.loc.gov/resource/g3814a.pm005050/

19 Library of Congress digital ID: www.loc.gov/resource/g3814a.pm005060/

20 Library of Congress digital ID: www.loc.gov/resource/g3814a.pm005050/

10 Centering and Multileveling Predictors

Purpose

Time to learn about three transformations of level-1 predictors. Grand-mean centering removes the overall mean value from the predictor. Group-mean centering removes the respective level-2 group mean from each level-1 predictor score. Finally, multileveling the predictor combines the group-mean-centered version of the level-1 predictor with a second version of the same predictor that uses level-2 averages. Each of these operations has implications for analyses, theories, or policy, and sometimes for all three.

To clarify these operations and their implications, we return to the cross-sectional dataset where individual rent observations are level 1 ($n = 132$), and neighborhoods – different sides of the board – are level 2 ($n = 4$). An empirical property-level variable undergoes these transformations.

Sometimes, centering and multileveling of level-1 predictors substantially alters impacts or interpretations of other model parameters. Two points prove crucial. (1) Group-mean centering creates a predictor with a different meaning (Raudenbush & Bryk, 2002, p. 31), thereby changing the underlying theory as well as the model being tested. "Centering around the group mean amounts to fitting a different model" (Kreft et al., 1995, abstract). (2) Multileveling similarly modifies both model and underlying theory. When a level-1 predictor is multileveled, the operation introduces a new level-2 impact pathway to the model as well as a new level-2 dynamic to the theory.

Implications follow for interpreting articles reporting multilevel-model results. Pay close attention to reported centering operations. Sometimes published researchers are not aware they have fitted a different model.

Overview

A new empirical variable is introduced. It undergoes three different transformations: grand mean centering, group mean centering, and multileveling. The how, why, and implications of each transformation are noted. Then the new

DOI: 10.4324/9781003392682-10

empirical variable, in various forms, is added to a cross-sectional ANCOVA rent prediction model.

A New Property-Level Variable

Given the rules of the game and the behavior of dice, scholars have modeled mathematically the chances of landing on each space on the Monopoly® board (Abbott & Richey, 1997; Stewart, 1996). Abbott and Richey (1997) captured these chances with a landing probability variable. They used percentages, so all the landing probabilities for all the spaces on the board added to 100%. Their landing probability values appear in Table 10.1. Analyses use only values for developable properties ($n = 22$).

These property-level values are applied to each level-1, individual rent observation ($n = 132$) in the Chapter 10 do file. After entering the variable (probab), each landing probability is multiplied by 1,000 to create a new variable (probab2). For models using probab2, a one-unit change equals an increase or decrease of one tenth of a percent.

Landing probabilities have implications for Monopoly game strategy. See Abbott and Richey (1997) for more details.

Questions Considered

Controlling for levels of development, do landing probability rent impacts depend on how the variable is transformed? Do various forms of the landing probability variable affect other model results? What are the implications for theory?

Analytic Approach

Four different forms of the landing probability variable appear in different cross-sectional ANCOVA models predicting individual rent values:

- The "plain" variable,
- A grand-mean-centered version,
- A group-mean-centered version, and
- A level-2 average appearing alongside the level-1 group-mean-centered version.

Individual rent values are the level-1 units, and the four sides of the board are level-2 units. The ANCOVA model structure parallels models shown in Chapter 7.

Table 10.1 Sorted list of values, Abbott and Richey's (1997) landing probability variable

Space	Name	Freq.(%)	Space	Name	Freq.(%)
10, 41, 42	Jail	11.724	29	Marvin Gardens	2.434
24	Illinois	2.990	14	Virginia	2.424
40	Go	2.907	34	Pennsylvania Ave	2.349
25	B&O RR	2.889	17	Comm. Chest 2	2.295
20	Free parking	2.826	35	Short Line RR	2.287
18	Tennessee	2.822	33	Comm. Chest 3	2.224
19	New York	2.809	4	Income tax	2.187
5	Reading RR	2.797	8	Vermont	2.179
16	St. James	2.681	13	States Ave	2.171
28	Water Works	2.650	9	Connecticut	2.163
15	Pennsylvania RR	2.633	6	Oriental	2.124
21	Kentucky	2.611	37	Park Place	2.057
12	Electric Company	2.610	38	Luxury tax	2.047
23	Indiana	2.563	3	Baltic	2.034
11	St. Charles	2.550	1	Mediterranean	2.005
26	Atlantic	2.536	2	Comm. Chest 1	1.769
31	Pacific	2.519	22	Chance 2	1.045
27	Ventnor	2.515	36	Chance 3	0.815
39	Boardwalk	2.480	7	Chance 1	0.814
32	North Carolina	2.468	30	Policeman	0.000

Source: Table 3, Abbott, S. D., & Richey, M. (1997). Take a walk on the Boardwalk. *The College Mathematics Journal*, 28(3), 162–171. https://doi.org/10.2307/2687519. Copyright © 1997 Mathematical Association of America, reprinted by permission of Taylor & Francis Ltd, www.tandfonline.com, on behalf of Mathematical Association of America, and with permission of the authors.

Note: These are percentages; for example 2.99% = .0299. Values for the variable used in analyses were multiplied by 1,000. Therefore, a one unit change in the variable used here reflects a change of 1/10th of a percent. The landing probability values added to the data file include only spaces with property deeds where player can add houses and hotels.

Centering and Multileveling Predictors

The operations discussed here, centering and multileveling of level-1 predictors, have analytic, empirical, and theoretical implications. Some of those implications get complicated and are skipped here.[1] Starting with the basics, how does each transform work?

What Is Centering?

A predictor in a statistical model is centered when its scores are rearranged so they center on a specific value, usually the mean predictor score. Centering is accomplished by subtracting the mean score from each individual score. This operation is also called de-meaning.

Broadly speaking, in a cross-sectional dataset with individuals nested within social or organizational contexts, centering operations "affect inferences for five purposes: [1] estimating fixed level-1 coefficients; [2] disentangling person-level and compositional effects; [3] estimating level-2 effects while adjusting for level-1 covariates; [4] estimating the variances of level-1 coefficients; and [5] estimating random level-1 coefficients" (Raudenbush & Bryk, 2002, p. 134). *Which* mean is removed determines whether the operation is grand-mean centering or group-mean centering.

Grand-Mean Centering

Idea and Operation

Grand-mean-centering a level-1 predictor subtracts its overall average score, its grand mean ($X..$), from individual scores (X_{ij}). The grand-mean-centered variable now averages zero.

$$\text{Grand-mean-centered level-1 predictor} = X_{ij} - X.. \qquad \text{(Eq. 10.1)}$$

In a one-way ANCOVA multilevel model with random effects and just one grand-mean-centered level-1 covariate, the level-1 equation becomes (Raudenbush & Bryk, 2002, p. 25, Eq. 2.13):

$$Y_{ij} = B_{0j} + B_{1j}(X_{ij} - X..) + r_{ij} \qquad \text{(Eq. 10.2: Raudenbush and Bryk's (2002) Eq. 2.13)}$$

With all predictors grand-mean centered, at both levels 1 and 2, the overall intercept (γ_{00}) reflects the average outcome score for an average level-1 unit in an average level-2 context. Stated differently, the intercept reflects the most likely outcome score after grand-mean-centering all predictors. The discussion here focuses specifically on level-1 predictors. One may center on a value other than the grand mean (Hox, 2010, p. 61).

Utility

Grand-mean centering of level-1 predictors is "often useful" (Raudenbush & Bryk, 2002, p. 33) for interpretive, evaluative, and theoretical purposes in a number of situations.

First, if zero is *not* a "legitimate, observable value" for *any* of your predictors, at either level 1 or level 2, then "the value of the intercept [in your model] is meaningless" (Hox, 2010, p. 61). To make it interpretable, grand-mean-center predictors.

> If we apply grand mean centering [to all of our predictors], we solve the problem because now the intercept in the regression equation is always interpretable as the expected value of the outcome variable, when all explanatory variables have their mean value.
>
> (Hox, 2010, p. 61)

Second, grand-mean-centering all predictors makes model variances more interpretable. "Variances of the intercept and the slopes now have a clear interpretation. They are the expected variances when all explanatory variables are equal to zero, in other words: the expected variances for the 'average' subject" (Hox et al., 2018, p. 48).

Third, if the model includes interactions, grand-mean-centering predictors facilitates interpreting the coefficients for interaction terms (Hox, 2010, pp. 62–68). The *b* weight linked to the interaction reflects the moderating impact for cases with average scores on the constituent variables of the interaction term. For more on centering and cross-level interaction effects in an ANCOVA multilevel model, see Snijders and Bosker (2012, p. 81).

That said, the advisability of centering before creating product-term interactions is an active area of research in monolevel models. Sometimes the impacts of centering the constituent terms in the interaction are not straightforward (Iacobucci et al., 2016; Olvera Astivia & Kroc, 2019). This work likely has implications of centering constituent variables in an interaction term in a multilevel model.

Fourth, grand-mean centering proves useful "in organizational research" if the purpose "is simply to estimate the association between a level-2 predictor [like a treatment delivered at the organization level] and the mean of *Y*, adjusting for one or more level-1 [causally linked] covariates" (Raudenbush & Bryk, 2002, p. 142). The utility accrues *only* when "there is no compositional effect" (Raudenbush & Bryk, 2002, p. 142), that is, no linkage between other level-1 factors, beyond the critical covariate, and the outcome. In this situation – a level-2 treatment, a level-1 causally relevant covariate like a pretest score for an educational outcome, and no differences in the composition of level-1 units across level-2 groups – *group*-mean centering (see next section) "*would be inappropriate*" (Raudenbush & Bryk, 2002, p. 142 emphasis added), but *grand*-mean centering would be helpful. With the latter transformation, "the estimate of the effect of *W* [the level 2 predictor] will be adjusted for differences between organizations [level 2 contexts] in the mean of *X*, the level-1 explanatory variable" (Raudenbush & Bryk, 2002, p. 142 emphasis added). See Raudenbush and Bryk (2002, pp. 111–112) for a classroom program effects example.

Fifth, turning to neighborhood research, investigators often struggle to separate the influence of neighborhood effects – ecological dynamics grounded in localized social, institutional, and cultural processes (Sharkey & Faber, 2014) – from the influence of other processes connected to variations across neighborhoods in the demographic composition of residents (Sampson et al., 2002). *Grand*-mean centering of predictors may help accomplish such separation. *Group*-mean centering will not.

Sixth, grand-mean centering *might* reduce the correlations among predictors, which in turn *might* decrease chances that strong correlations among predictors create multicollinearity problems. Familiar multicollinearity diagnostics available in monolevel models – tolerances, variance inflation factors, correlations between estimated coefficients, and inflated standard errors of parameter estimates – all can be examined (Hamilton, 1992, pp. 133–137). "High standard errors are a principal symptom of multicollinearity. They indicate that coefficient estimates are imprecise – expected to vary widely across different samples" (Hamilton, 1992, pp. 134–135).

These same examinations also may help diagnose multilevel models where multicollinearity can create "estimates [that] will be misleading" (Shieh & Fouladi, 2003, p. 983) and lead to "standard errors of . . . the coefficients . . . to be inflated" (Shieh & Fouladi, 2003, p. 983). A novel impact in the multilevel context is that multicollinearity can bias components of the estimated variance-covariance matrix for random parameters (Shieh & Fouladi, 2003, p. 982). The biasing of the latter estimates introduced by the multicollinearity "is not unidirectional but can result in either attenuation or inflation of the true effect" (Shieh & Fouladi, 2003, p. 983). To sum up on this last point: grand-mean centering may assist with multicollinearity, but multicollinearity impacts in multilevel models may go beyond those seen in monolevel models.

Group-Mean Centering

Idea and Operation

Here, the mean subtracted from each level-1 predictor score is not the overall mean ($X..$). Instead, it is the level-2 mean predictor score ($X_{.j}$) for the specific group in which the level-1 predictor score is nested.

$$\text{Group-mean-centered level-1 predictor} = X_{ij} - X_{.j} \qquad \text{(Eq. 10.3)}$$

This is also called "centering within context" (Kreft et al., 1995, p. 2) or "centering on the group mean . . . centering on the group mean makes very explicit that the individual scores should be interpreted relative to their group's mean" (Hox, 2010, p. 7). Consequently, predictor scores become localized, within-group comparisons.

Predictor means, overall and within each group, are affected. The overall average predictor score becomes zero, as does the predictor mean within *each* level-2 group. Because the group-mean-centered predictor discards all between-group differences on the predictor, in cases where the raw predictor contained notable between-group variation, impacts of the raw versus group-mean-centered predictor will look different (Kreft et al., 1995).

It is crucial to understand the theoretical shift created with this centering operation. It not only constructs a new variable, it forms a new underlying theoretical concept.

Consider, for example, a multi-neighborhood survey of urban residents in one city predicting reactions to crime like personal safety concerns, and using perceptions of crime risk as a predictor (Wyant, 2008). With the raw predictor, or the grand-mean-centered predictor, an average score on perceived risk typifies the entire, citywide sample. Above-average raw or grand mean perceived risk scores are higher than typical for the same entire sample. In contrast, after group mean centering perceived risk, average scores become context-specific. Average perceived risk is now typical *only* for the specific neighborhood where the respondent lives. A respondent with an above average group-mean-centered score perceives more risk than a typical respondent in his/her/their *specific* neighborhood.

In educational outcome research, the late Lee Cronbach argued in the 1970s that group-mean centering usefully separates between-classroom effects, arising, for example, from teacher differences, from within-classroom effects, arising, for example, from within-group student differences (Cronbach, 1976; Cronbach & Webb, 1975). Within-classroom effects in educational psychology represent one example of a broader phenomenon known as frog-pond effects (Shinn, 1990). Variables capturing frog-pond effects depict how each record, each frog, stacks up against the other records in the same group, that is, the other frogs in *that specific pond.*

> This means that for a medium-sized frog the effect of being in a pond filled with big frogs is different than [the effect of] being [a medium-sized frog] in a pond filled with small frogs . . . the frog pond effect states that the effect of [pupil] intelligence on school success depends on the relative standing of the pupils in their own class.
>
> (Hox et al., 2018, p. 50)

Utility

Group-mean centering of level-1 predictors proves useful on several counts. Perhaps most importantly, restricting predictor variation to within-context variation may help better align the indicator with the proposed theoretical construct and its predicted impacts. This is [2] in Raudenbush and Bryk's

(2002) list of purposes. Wyant (2008), discussed previously, was interested in relative differences between neighbors in perceived crime risk. For "perceptions of crime risk . . . those seeing a bigger crime problem than their neighbors were more afraid" (Wyant, 2008, p. 52).

Second, group-mean centering permits multileveling a level-1 predictor. The multileveling is explained shortly, but the key idea is that researchers' theoretical models may include *both* hypothesized level-2 predictor dynamics as well as hypothesized level-1 predictor dynamics. "When group-mean centering is chosen . . . the relationship between X_{ij} and Y_{ij} is directly decomposed into its within- and between-group components" (Raudenbush & Bryk, 2002, p. 141). For example, researchers studying math achievement may seek to separate impacts of within-school student SES differences from between-school impacts of average student SES (Raudenbush & Bryk, 2002, pp. 139–141). Returning to Wyant's (2008, p. 46) study of fear of crime, ecological impacts of "shared views on crime risk" were of interest alongside individual-within-neighborhood differences in perceived crime risk. The theoretical model tested included two perceived risk dynamics, one social psychological, one ecological.

Third, as with grand-mean centering, group-mean centering may improve the interpretability of the overall intercept and the level-2 intercepts. For example, for a residents-clustered-by-neighborhoods survey sample in one city, if all level-1 predictors are group-mean centered, and there are no level-2 predictors, the overall intercept and the level-2 intercepts reflect expected scores for respondents who are typical of their respective neighborhood contexts.

A fourth advantage is that group-mean centering, like grand-mean centering, may reduce multicollinearity among level-1 predictors.

Disadvantages

With group-mean-centered level-1 predictors, one cannot directly estimate between-group, level-2 predictor impacts if the level-1 predictor scores in raw form vary across level-2 groups (Raudenbush & Bryk, 2002, p. 142). *Group-mean-centered predictors cannot remove between-context compositional differences because in each context the average score on the group-mean-centered predictor is zero.* Thus, with group-mean-centered level-1 predictors, one cannot directly estimate *net* neighborhood effects, or level-2 effects more broadly, while controlling for level-1 compositional differences.[2]

Time, Group-Mean Centering, and Longitudinal Data

Raudenbush and Bryk (2002, p. 33) note that "specialized choices of [the centering] location for X [a level-1 predictor] are often sensible" even if those choices are not the group mean or the grand mean. They specifically reference group-mean centering with longitudinal data.

As noted in Chapter 9, for longitudinal growth studies, data are often arranged such that the level-1 units are occasions and the level-2 units are persons. The investigator may wish to define a metric of the level-1 predictors such that the intercept is the expected outcome for person *i* at a specific time point of theoretical interest, for example, age at entering school. As long as the data encompass the time point used for the centered predictor value of 0, such an intercept is appropriate (Raudenbush & Bryk, 2002, p. 33).

Last Thoughts on Group-Mean Centering

Group-mean centering, like grand-mean centering, has its detractors as well as its proponents. Costs versus benefits of this operation continue to be actively researched and debated (Kelley et al., 2017; Paccagnella, 2006). Nevertheless, when considering whether to group-mean-center level-1 predictors, keep these four points in mind. (1) The transformation creates a new indicator for a new concept. (2) Be sure the new concept, and the dynamic that links the new concept to the outcome, makes sense *theoretically*. (3) If the group-mean-centered version of the variable has a markedly lower impact than the raw variable, this means noticeable, outcome-relevant, between-group variation in the predictor has been discarded. Consider introducing a level-2 version of the raw predictor to recapture that variation. Do so, however, only if it makes sense theoretically. (4) In a cross-sectional file with records clustered by organizations or groups or places, group-mean-centered predictors cannot control for level-1 compositional differences across groups. Solid researchers publishing in good journals sometimes get confused on this point. Don't be.

Multileveling Level-1 Predictors

"Group mean centering and adding the group mean as a predictor variable is most useful when the research question requires a clear separation of individual and group" impacts of a predictor (Hox et al., 2018, p. 51). As noted previously in the Wyant (2008) example, he explored perceived risk dynamics *at multiple levels*.

Theoretical Separation of Distinct Dynamics at Distinct Levels

As noted previously, a group-mean-centered level-1 predictor $(X_{ij} - X_{.j})$ captures within-group frog-pond effects. If raw or grand-mean-centered level-1 predictor scores are aggregated to level 2, those level-2 averages $(X_{.j})$ capture between-group effects at level 2. If both versions of the predictor are included in the same model – group-mean-centered level-1 scores, and level-2 averages – impacts of two distinct constructs operating at two distinct levels can be examined. The two predictors will be completely uncorrelated. Supporting multilevel theoretical dynamics are required.

Considering Multilevel Impacts of Landing Probabilities

What happens if Abbott and Richey's (1997) landing probability variable is multileveled? The group-mean-centered values would examine frog-pond effects. Are rents higher for properties with higher landing probabilities than other properties in the same neighborhood? Neighborhood-level landing probability averages provide insight into ecological rent impacts. Level-2 landing probability rent impacts would shed light on potential game inequalities, built in across the four sides of the playing board, by game designers. If landing probabilities are lower on some sides of the board compared to others, and if those neighborhood landing probability differentials link to higher or lower rents, then owning properties on certain sides of the board would carry built-in advantages or disadvantages.

See Figure 10.1. It illustrates a model of multilevel impacts of landing probabilities on rent.

An Empirical Example

This section illustrates what centering and multileveling does to Abbott and Richey's (1997) landing probability variable. The raw, grand-mean-centered, and group-mean-centered probability variable is examined graphically using clustered box-and-whisker plots. Then, descriptive statistics are scrutinized. Finally, ANCOVA model results using different versions of the variable are

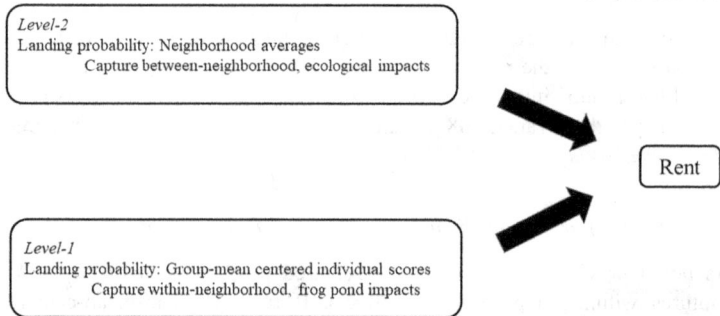

> Level-2
> Landing probability: Neighborhood averages
>   Capture between-neighborhood, ecological impacts

Rent

> Level-1
> Landing probability: Group-mean centered individual scores
>   Capture within-neighborhood, frog pond impacts

Figure 10.1 Hypothesized multilevel net impacts of landing probabilities on rent. The two predictors correlate zero. The model controls for levels of real estate development (not shown).

inspected. Of particular interest is how model fit, intercepts, and *b* weights may vary across models with different versions of the landing variable.

Graphical Inspection Via Box-and-Whisker Plots

Figure 10.2 shows distributions of scaled-up landing probabilities, separately by sides of the playing board, before any centering operations. It suggests some inequalities across different sides of the playing board.

On the first side of the board, landing probabilities appear markedly lower.[3] Further, landing chances on the fourth side of the board seem lower than on the second and third sides. The second side of the board, between Jail and Free Parking, had the widest interquartile range and the highest median landing probability, around 2.6%.

Figure 10.3 shows neighborhood distributions of scaled-up landing probabilities after grand-mean-centering the level-1 variable. With grand-mean centering, the average level-1 value for the variable, 24.31, is removed from each record.

Except for the change in values on the horizontal axis, Figure 10.3 replicates Figure 10.2 showing the untransformed variable. The average value, as shown by the vertical reference line, is now zero. Scores range from −4.26 to 5.59. The four different box-and-whisker plots hold the same positions relative to one another as they did in the preceding figure.

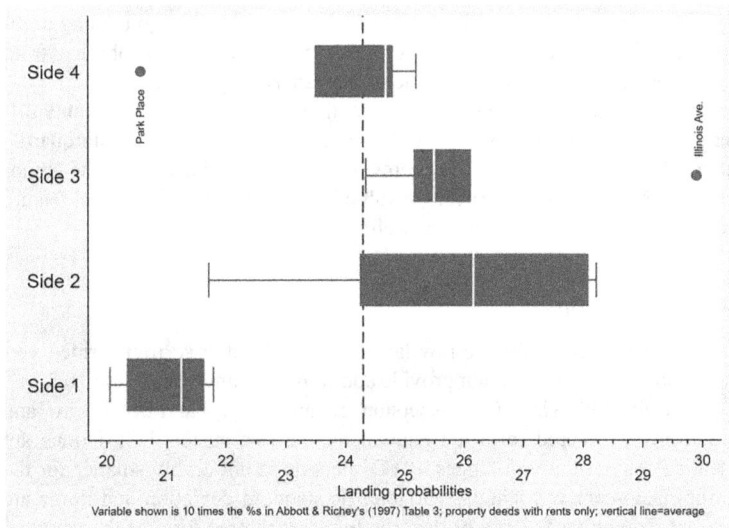

Figure 10.2 Scaled-up landing probability variable: box-and-whisker plots for each side of the playing board.

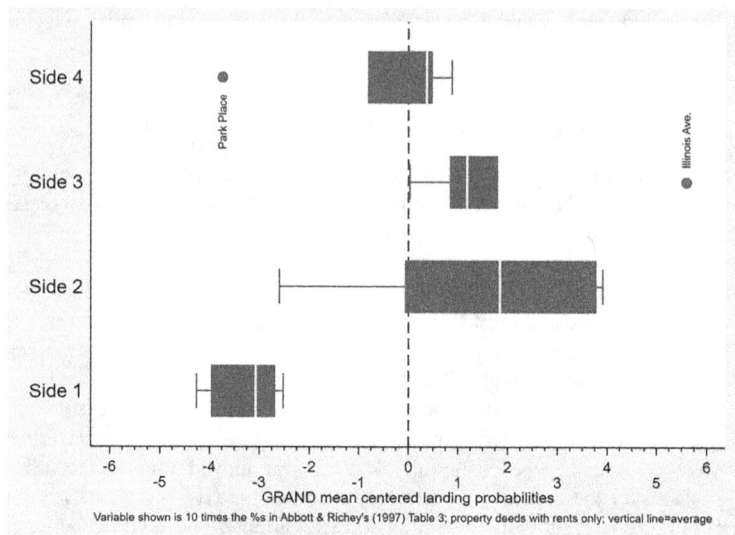

Figure 10.3 Grand-mean-centered, scaled-up landing probability variable: box-and-whisker plots for each side of the playing board.

Figure 10.4 shows neighborhood distributions of scaled-up landing probabilities after group-mean-centering. This centering operation subtracts from each score the average level-1 value of its respective group mean.

In group-mean-centered form, the landing variable looks remarkably different. Between-group average differences have disappeared. Interquartile ranges for all four neighborhoods now overlap substantially. As in the grand-mean-centered version, the average value is zero. The important novel feature is that each group mean is zero as well.

Descriptive Statistics

Descriptive statistics for the raw landing variable, its two transformed versions, and the level-2 version provide additional insights. See Table 10.2.

Note the following: (1) Dispersion of landing probabilities in raw and grand-mean-centered form are equivalent; the two standard deviations are identical, as are the two ranges. (2) Dispersion is noticeably smaller for the group-mean-centered landing variable; its standard deviation and range are smaller than either the raw or the grand-mean-centered form of the variable.

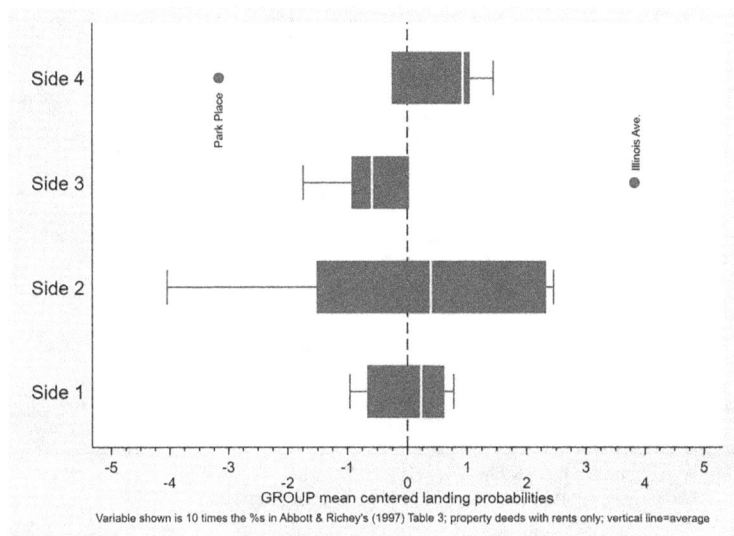

Figure 10.4 Group-mean-centered, scaled-up landing probability variable: box-and-whisker plots for each side of the playing board.

Variance after group-mean centering is less than half of the original value.[4] This suggests that a considerable amount of between-group variation in the original variable was removed with the group-mean centering operation. (3) Level-2 neighborhood average landing probabilities have a smaller range than all other versions of the variable. This is no surprise since the variable is built from four averages. Its dispersion is larger than the group-mean-centered version but smaller than the raw and grand-mean-centered versions.

Results: Predicting Rent With Different Versions of Landing Probabilities Variables

Table 10.3 displays results from six different multilevel models predicting rent: the null model (ANOVA); the ANCOVA model controlling for levels of real estate development; a model adding the plain landing-probabilities variable (Plain LP); one adding a grand-mean-centered version of these probabilities (Grand C LP); one adding a group-mean-centered version of the probabilities (Group C LP); and one adding both a group-mean-centered version and a level-2 version (LP L1+L2). What do results reveal?

Table 10.2 Abbott and Richey's (1997) landing probabilities variable: Descriptive
statistics

Variable	Landing probabilities	Landing probabilities: Grand mean centered	Landing probabilities: Group mean centered	Neighborhood average (level-2) landing probabilities
Variable name	probab2	c_grand_p	c_group_p	nblandav
Statistic				
N	132	132	132	132
Min	20.05	−4.261	−4.052	21.01
Max	29.9	5.589	3.818	26.082
Mean	24.311	0	0	24.311
SD	2.662	2.662	1.754	2.002
Median (p50)	24.74	0.429	−0.114	25.762
Range	9.85	9.85	7.87	5.072

Source: Abbott, S. D., & Richey, M. (1997). Take a walk on the Boardwalk. *The College Mathematics Journal, 28*(3), 162–171. https://doi.org/10.2307/2687519. Table 3.

Note: Only landing probabilities associated with a rent-generating property deed entered. These 22 values were replicated across the 6 rents for each property (level 1 $n = 132$). Level 2 = four sides of the playing board. Original landing probability values have been multiplied by 1,000; i.e., percentage values multiplied by 10. With the scaled up probabilities 1 unit change = 1/10th of a percent.

Lines 1–8 show the familiar positive significant impacts of guesthouses and hotels on rent.

Lines 9–12 from the plain LP model show that each tenth of a percent increase in these probabilities is estimated to elevate rent $7.98, controlling for levels of real estate development. Likelier-to-land places do charge slightly higher rents.

Lines 13–16 from the grand-mean-centered model show the exact same net rent impact of landing probabilities as seen with the raw version of the predictor.

Lines 17–20 show predictor net rent impacts for group-mean-centered landing probabilities. The landing probability net rent impact is reduced about 17% after removing between-neighborhood differences in landing probabilities.[5] Each tenth of a percent increase in landing probabilities is now estimated to elevate rent $6.61.

Lines 21–24 show impacts of neighborhood-average landing probabilities. A tenth of a percent increase is estimated to elevate rents $47.47. Descriptively, the estimated between-group net rent impact of neighborhood-average landing probabilities is larger than the estimated within-neighborhood net impact.

Table 10.3 Rent impacts of landing probabilities (LP) controlling for levels of development: un-centered (Plain LP), grand mean centered (Grand C LP), group mean centered (Group C LP), and multileveled (LP L1+L2)

Model	ANOVA	ANCOVA	Plain LP	Grand C LP	Group C LP	LP L1+L2
Predictor						
N of guesthouses present						
1	$215.786	$215.786	$215.786	$215.786	$215.786	$215.786
2	($12.236)	($12.236)	($12.211)	($12.211)	($12.210)	($12.210)
3	17.636	17.636	17.671	17.671	17.673	17.673
4	p < .001	p < .001	p < .001	p < .001	p < .001	p < .001
Hotel present (1) or not (0)						
5	$1,060.518	$1,060.518	$1,060.518	$1,060.518	$1,060.518	$1,060.518
6	($48.942)	($48.942)	($48.845)	($48.845)	($48.840)	($48.840)
7	21.669	21.669	21.712	21.712	21.714	21.714
8	p < .001	p < .001	p < .001	p < .001	p < .001	p < .001
Landing probability 1 unit change = one tenth of a percent						
9			$7.982			
10			($8.867)			
11			0.900			
12			ns			
Grand mean centered landing probability 1 unit change = one tenth of a percent						
13				$7.982		
14				($8.867)		
15				0.900		
16				ns		
Group mean centered by side of board landing probability 1 unit change = one tenth of a percent						
17					$6.610	$6.610
18					($9.019)	($9.019)
19					0.733	0.733
20					ns	ns

(Continued)

Table 10.3 (Continued)

Model	ANOVA	ANCOVA	Plain LP	Grand C LP	Group C LP	LP L1+L2
	Neighborhood level average landing probability					
21						$47.470
22						($44.197)
23						1.074
24						ns
25 Intercept	$469.124	-$67.265	-$286.859	-$50.592	-$52.475	-$1,065.043
26	($100.569)	($104.549)	($239.508)	($105.682)	($109.185)	($1,151.246)
Random effects parameters						
27 var(_cons)	$35,277.262	$40,120.580	$37,283.345	$37,283.336	$40,125.454	$30,918.046
28	($28,910.565)	($29,137.704)	($27,280.797)	($27,280.787)	($29,137.937)	($22,612.509)
29 var(e)	$169,677.210	$32,936.236	$32,804.609	$32,804.609	$32,798.559	$32,798.455
30	($21,216.497)	($4,117.279)	($4,101.565)	($4,101.566)	($4,100.067)	($4,100.041)
Model parameters						
31 N of observations	132	132	132	132	132	132
32 Log likelihood	-986.17	-881.28	-880.88	-880.88	-881.01	-880.51
33 AIC	1,978.33	1,772.56	1,773.77	1,773.77	1,774.03	1,775.01
34 BIC	1,986.98	1,786.98	1,791.06	1,791.06	1,791.33	1,795.19
35 Wald χ^2 model test		531.21	534.16	534.16	533.98	535.14
36 Model test p-value		$p < .001$	$p < .001$	$p < .001$	$p < .001$	$p < .001$
37 N RE parameters	2.00	2.00	2.00	2.00	2.00	2.00
38 N variances	2.00	2.00	2.00	2.00	2.00	2.00

Note: Standard errors in parentheses. For predictors, rows show b/(se)/t / $p <$. Level-1 = individual rent value ($n = 132$); level-2 = four sides of playing board ($n = 4$). var(_cons) = Level-2 residual variance. var(e) = Level-1 residual variance. L1 + L2 = group mean centered + level-2 Impacts of n_house and hotel not shown.

Pause and reflect a moment. For the landing probabilities variable, descriptively, the between-group slope and the within-group slope are different. Descriptively, multilevel impacts are occurring.

Lines 27–28 describe the variance of the level-2 rent residuals. Descriptively, it is lowest, $30,918, in the model allowing both level-1 and level-2 rent impacts of landing probabilities. Note, for some of these models, aforementioned negative level-2 R^2 problems appear.

Lines 29–30 show the variation in level-1 rent residuals. The amount is comparable in all the models with predictors, slightly below $33,000.

Lines 33–34 show AIC and BIC values. The BIC value is at least 4 lower for the ANCOVA model (1,786.98) compared to all the other ones. If one were using BIC values to decide, statistically, which model best fits the data after controlling for model complexity, the ANCOVA model *without* landing probability variables would be recommended.

Apply this model selection choice based on BIC values to the question posed earlier. Were game designers somehow biasing the game in favor of more expensive properties by making landing probabilities higher on sides of the board where rents were higher? The noticeably lower BIC value for the ANCOVA rent model *without* a landing probability variable says no, they were not. The landing probability variable, in various level-1 forms, or entered as predictors at multiple levels, does not help explain rent values once development and random variation across neighborhoods have been considered.

Closing Thoughts

1. Think carefully about centering choices. What makes sense theoretically? What might help with analytic challenges like multicollinearity?
2. What are typical choices? Often researchers will either (a) grand-mean-center everything or just about everything; or (b) grand-mean-center at level 2 and group-mean-center at level 1. Both choices are justifiable. Which to choose depends on your purposes.
3. Other centering choices, or not centering at all, also can be justified theoretically and practically.
4. Group-mean centering of a level-1 predictor changes the meaning of the variable. Have a theoretical construct and an aligning theoretical dynamic to explain how this frog-pond-effects variable can shape the outcome.
5. The same point applies when constructing a level-2 version of a group-mean-centered level-1 predictor. Have an aligning theoretical construct and related theoretical dynamic.
6. Turning individual-level predictors into level-2 context variables is a tricky business, and one risks running afoul of the contextual fallacy (Hauser, 1970, 1974; Taylor, 2015, pp. 90–93). There are methodological, analytic, and theoretical aspects to be considered if this fallacy is to be avoided.

152   *Centering and Multileveling Predictors*

7. Group-mean centering of level-1 predictors, in a cross-sectional file with records clustered by organizations or groups or places, will *not* control for compositional differences across level-2 units.

8. The analytic consequences of centering predictors in multilevel models are an active area of scholarship and debate.

Notes

1 The consequences as well as the advantages and disadvantages of different centering operations in monolevel and multilevel models with different types of connections between predictors and outcomes rapidly becomes technical and beyond the introductory intent of the current volume. "The technical details that govern the relations between [multilevel-model] parameter estimates using raw scores, grand mean centered scores, and group mean scores, are complicated" (Hox et al., 2018, p. 50). For more details, see references suggested by Hox et al. (2018, p. 50). In the case of RCR models, see Snijders and Bosker (2012, pp. 87–89). Discussion here considers centering *only* in the context of a multilevel ANCOVA model initially including only level-1 predictors.

2 It may be possible, however, to estimate net neighborhood effects *indirectly*. See Raudenbush and Bryk's (2002, p. 140, Table 5.11) between-classroom example.

3 One could confirm the second point by running the monolevel model `regress probab2 i.sidezero`.

4 The ratio of the variance of the group-mean-centered version to the original version is $(1.754^2/2.662^2) = .43$.

5 $(1-(6.610/7.982))$.

11 Next Steps

This book has deployed data taken from the property deeds in the classic US 65th Anniversary Edition of the board game Monopoly®. Two additional variables – one hypothetical, one empirical – supplemented property deed development and rent data. These data powered examples of five types of multilevel models: ANOVA with no predictors, ANCOVA with fixed level-1 predictors, RCR allowing varying impacts of one level-1 predictor, a longitudinal model allowing fixed and varying impacts of time, and ANCOVA models with centered and multileveled level-1 predictors.

Those who comprehend these models as they apply to these data, warts and all, should move next to more complex longitudinal or cross-sectional datasets of interest. Work through the applicable models demonstrated here. Start with monolevel and multilevel ANOVA models. Then construct monolevel and multilevel ANCOVA models. Check model details. Adapt relevant code snippets from the online files.

If all that works out, start grappling with more complex multilevel models. Are your outcomes binary (Rabe-Hesketh & Skrondal, 2012b, Chapter 10), counts (Rabe-Hesketh & Skrondal, 2012b, Chapter 13; Sorg & Taylor, 2011), ordered categories (Blasko et al., 2015; Rabe-Hesketh & Skrondal, 2012b, Chapter 11), or unordered categories (Johnson et al., 2015; Skrondal & Rabe-Hesketh, 2003)? Multilevel models can address each of these. Are data nested at three levels (Rabe-Hesketh & Skrondal, 2012a, Chapter 8)? Or do you need a three-level model with a measurement level underneath a two-level persons-in-neighborhood data structure (Sampson et al., 1997)? Does the clustering involve cross-classification (Lockwood, 2012; Rabe-Hesketh & Skrondal, 2012b)? Most importantly, build on the understanding gained here. Start simple, progressively elaborate, checking key details along the way.

Multilevel models are just one tool among many in the quantitative toolbox. They are no better or worse than other types of quantitative analytics. Just different.

But also the same. Multilevel models overlap in interesting ways with structural equation models and mediating models (Preacher et al., 2010), as well as meta-analyses (Boele et al., 2019; Van Den Noortgate et al., 2015;

DOI: 10.4324/9781003392682-11

Weisz et al., 2013). Figuring out which specific research questions are best examined with multilevel models is an ongoing process.

Reading more deeply should help. Staying close to Stata, Rabe-Hesketh and Skrondal's two volumes (2012a, 2012b) are detailed and comprehensive. If you are just thinking about learning more about how these models work and the ideas behind them, several works would assist (Hox, 2010; Hox et al., 2018; Raudenbush & Bryk, 2002; Snijders & Bosker, 2012). If R is of interest, Gelman and Hill (2007) cover both regression and multilevel models using that package. If seeking code for a wide range of models using different programs – SPSS, SAS, R, Stata, HLM – Garson (2019) may prove useful. If looking for just one volume for learning next steps, consider Hox et al. (2018): solid, thoughtful, comprehensive, and less intimidating than other volumes.

In the mid-1990s, I started applying these tools to my research interests (Perkins & Taylor, 1996). I began teaching these tools to colleagues and graduate students in the late 1990s. I am still learning how these models can advance theory, policy, and practice, and how they are also limited. Be patient with yourself as you start your own journey. Monolevel land, or *Flatland* (Abbott et al., 2010), will never look the same.

References

Abbott, A. (1997). Seven types of ambiguity. *Theory and Society, 26*(2–3), 357–391.

Abbott, E. A., Lindgren, W. F., & Banchoff, T. F. (2010). *Flatland: An edition with notes and commentary.* Cambridge University Press.

Abbott, S. D., & Richey, M. (1997). Take a walk on the Boardwalk. *The College Mathematics Journal, 28*(3), 162–171. https://doi.org/10.2307/2687519

Acock, A. C. (2018). *A gentle introduction to Stata* (6th ed.). Stata Press.

Aiken, L. S., & West, S. G. (1991). *Multiple regression: Testing and interpreting interactions.* Sage.

Akaike, H. (1974). A new look at statistical model identification. *IEEE Transactions on Automatic Control, 19*(6), 716–723. https://doi.org/10.1109/TAC.1974.1100705

Akers, R. L., & Sellers, C. S. (2012). *Criminological theories* (6th ed.). Oxford University Press.

Allison, P. D. (2009). *Fixed effects regression analysis.* Sage.

Allison, P. D., & Waterman, R. P. (2002). Fixed-effects negative binomial regression models. *Sociological Methodology, 32*, 247–265.

Anselin, L. (1988). *Spatial econometrics: Methods and models.* Kluwer Academic.

Anselin, L. (1995). Local indicators of spatial association – LISA. *Geographical Analysis, 27*(2), 93–115. https://doi.org/10.1111/j.1538-4632.1995.tb00338.x

Auspurg, K., Brüderl, J., & Wöhler, T. (2019). Does immigration reduce the support for welfare spending? A cautionary tale on spatial panel data analysis. *American Sociological Review, 84*(4), 754–763. https://doi.org/10.1177/0003122419856347

Baller, R. D., Anselin, L., Messner, S. F., Deane, G., & Hawkins, D. F. (2001). Structural covariates of US county homicide rates: Incorporating spatial effects. *Criminology, 39*(3), 561–590.

Baron, R. M., & Kenny, D. A. (1986). The moderator-mediator variable distinction in social psychological research: Conceptual, strategic and statistical considerations. *Journal of Personality and Social Psychology, 51*, 1173–1182.

Baum, C. F. (2006). *An introduction to modern econometrics using STATA.* Stata Press.

Baumer, E. P., & Arnio, A. N. (2012). Multi-level modeling and criminological inquiry. In D. Gadd, S. Karstedt, & S. F. Messner (Eds.), *The SAGE handbook of criminological research methods* (pp. 97–110). Sage.

Belotti, F., Hughes, G., & Mortari, A. P. (2017). Spatial panel-data models using Stata. *The Stata Journal, 17*(1), 139–180. https://doi.org/10.1177/1536867x1701700109

Berk, R., Brown, L., & Zhao, L. (2009). Statistical inference after model selection. *Journal of Quantitative Criminology*, *26*(2), 217–236. https://doi.org/10.1007/s10940-009-9077-7

Bickel, R. (2006). *Multilevel analysis for applied research: It's just regression.* Guilford.

Blalock, H. M., Jr. (1963). Correlated independent variables: The problem of multicollinearity. *Social Forces*, *43*, 233–237.

Blalock, H. M., Jr. (1979). *Social statistics* (Rev. 2nd ed.). McGraw Hill.

Blasko, B. L., Roman, C. G., & Taylor, R. B. (2015). Local gangs and residents' perceptions of unsupervised teen groups: Implications for the incivilities thesis and neighborhood effects. *Journal of Criminal Justice*, *43*(1), 20–28. http://dx.doi.org/10.1016/j.jcrimjus.2014.11.002

Boele, S., Jolien Van der, G., Minet de, W., Inge, E. V. D. V., Crocetti, E., & Branje, S. (2019). Linking parent–child and peer relationship quality to empathy in adolescence: A multilevel meta-analysis. *Journal of Youth and Adolescence*, *48*(6), 1033–1055. https://doi.org/10.1007/s10964-019-00993-5

Boto-Garcia, D., Mariel, P., Banos Pino, J., & Alvarez, A. (2022). Tourists' willingness to pay for holiday trip characteristics: A discrete choice experiment. *Tourism Economics*, *28*(2), 349–370.

Browne, W. J., Goldstein, H., & Rabash, J. (2001). Multiple membership multiple classification (MMMC) models. *Statistical Modelling*, *1*, 103–124.

Browne, W. J., Lahi, M. G., Parker, R. M. A., & Charlton, C. (2023). *A guide to sample size calculations for random effects models via simulation and the MLPowSim software package.* University of Bristol, Centre for Multilevel Modeling. Retrieved February 20, 2023, from www.bristol.ac.uk/cmm/software/mlpowsim/

Bulmer, M. G. (1967). *Principles of statistics.* Dover Publications.

Burnham, K. P., & Anderson, D. R. (1998). *Model selection and inference: A practical information-theoretic approach.* Springer.

Cameron, A. C., & Trivedi, P. K. (2010). *Microeconometrics using Stata* (Rev. ed.). Stata Press.

Chaix, B., Merlo, J., & Chauvin, P. (2005). Comparison of a spatial approach with the multilevel approach for investigating place effects on health: The example of healthcare utilisation in France. *Journal of Epidemiology and Community Health*, *59*(6), 517–526. https://doi.org/10.1136/jech.2004.025478

Chambers, J. M., Cleveland, W. S., Kleiner, B., & Tukey, P. A. (1983). *Graphical methods for data analysis.* Wadsworth/Duxbury.

Choldin, H. M. (2019). Subcommunities: Neighborhoods and suburbs in sociological perspective. In M. Micklin & H. M. Choldin (Eds.), *Sociological human ecology* (pp. 237–276). Routledge. (Original work published 1984)

Choldin, H. M., Hanson, C., & Bohrer, R. (1980). Suburban status instability. *American Sociological Review*, *45*, 972–983.

Chou, C.-P., Bentler, P. M., & Pentz, M. A. (1998). Comparisons of two statistical approaches to study growth curves: The multilevel model and the latent curve analysis. *Structural Equation Modeling: A Multidisciplinary Journal*, *5*(3), 247–266.

Cliff, A. D., & Ord, K. (1970). Spatial autocorrelation: A review of existing and new measures with applications. *Economic Geography*, *46*, 269–292.

Collins, T. (2005). *Probabilities in the game of monopoly.* Retrieved February 16, 2018, from www.tkcs-collins.com/truman/monopoly/monopoly.shtml#Conclusions

Congdon, P. (2006). *Bayesian statistical modeling* (2nd ed.). Wiley.

Cronbach, L. J. (1976). *Research on classrooms and schools: Formulation of questions, design, and analysis.* Stanford Evaluation Consortium.

Cronbach, L. J., & Webb, N. (1975). Between-class and within-class effects in a reported aptitude treatment interaction: Reanalysis of a study by G. L. Anderson. *Journal of Educational Psychology, 67*(6), 717–724. https://doi.org/10.1037/0022-0663. 67.6.717

Darlington, R. B. (1990). *Regression and linear models.* McGraw Hill.

Diez Roux, A. V., & Mair, C. (2010). Neighborhoods and health. *Annals of the New York Academy of Sciences, 1186*(1), 125–145. https://doi.org/10.1111/j.1749-6632. 2009.05333.x

Dubin, R. A., & Goodman, A. C. (1982). Valuation of education and crime neighborhood characteristics through hedonic housing prices. *Population and Environment, 5,* 166–181.

Dubin, R. A., & Sung, C.-H. (1990). Specification of hedonic regressions: Non-nested tests on measures of neighborhood quality. *Journal of Urban Economics, 27*(1), 97–110. https://doi.org/10.1016/0094-1190(90)90027-K

Duncan, T. E., Duncan, S. C., Strycker, L. A., Li, F., & Alpert, A. (1999). *An introduction to latent variable growth curve modeling.* Lawrence Erlbaum.

Entwisle, B. (2007). Putting people into place. *Demography, 44*(4), 687–703.

Finch, W. H., Bolin, J. E., & Kelley, K. (2019). *Multilevel modeling using R* (2nd ed.). CRC Press.

Fine, A., Moule, R., Trinkner, R., Frick, P. J., Steinberg, L., & Cauffman, E. (2021). Legal socialization and individual belief in the code of the streets: A theoretical integration and longitudinal test. *Justice Quarterly,* 1–22. https://doi.org/10.1080/0741 8825.2021.1944285

Freedman, D. A. (2006). On the so-called "Huber sandwich estimator" and "Robust standard errors". *The American Statistician, 60*(4), 299–302.

Gans, H. J. (1967). *The Levittowners.* Pantheon.

Garson, G. D. (2019). *Multilevel modeling: Applications in STATA, IBM SPSS, SAS, R, and HLM.* Sage.

Gelman, A. (2018). The failure of null hypothesis significance testing when studying incremental changes, and what to do about it. *Personality and Social Psychology Bulletin, 44*(1), 16–23. https://doi.org/10.1177/0146167217729162

Gelman, A., Carlin, J. B., Stern, H. S., & Rubin, D. B. (2004). *Bayesian data analysis* (2nd ed.). Chapman & Hall/CRC.

Gelman, A., & Hill, J. (2007). *Data analysis using regression and multilevel/hierarchi cal models.* Cambridge University Press.

Gordon, R. A. (1968). Issues in multiple regression. *American Journal of Sociology, 73,* 592–616.

Hamilton, L. C. (1992). *Regression with graphics.* Brooks/Cole.

Hannon, L., & Knapp, P. (2003). Reassessing nonlinearity in the urban disadvantage/ violent crime relationship: An example of methodological bias from log transformation. *Criminology, 41*(4), 1427–1448. https://doi.org/10.1111/j.1745-9125.2003. tb01026.x

Hauser, R. M. (1970). Context and consex: A cautionary tale. *American Journal of Sociology, 75*(4), 645–664.

Hauser, R. M. (1974). Contextual analysis revisited. *Sociological Methods & Research, 2*(3), 365–375. https://doi.org/10.1177/004912417400200305

158 References

Haviland, A., Nagin, D. S., & Rosenbaum, P. R. (2007). Combining propensity score matching and group-based trajectory analysis in an observational study. *Psychological Methods, 12*(3), 247–267. https://doi.org/10.1037/1082-989x.12.3.247

Hipp, J. R., & Wickes, R. (2017). Violence in urban neighborhoods: A longitudinal study of collective efficacy and violent crime. *Journal of Quantitative Criminology, 33*(4), 783–808. https://doi.org/10.1007/s10940-016-9311-z

Hox, J. J. (2010). *Multilevel analysis* (2nd ed.). Routledge.

Hox, J. J., Moerbeck, M., & van de Schoot, R. (2018). *Multilevel analysis: Techniques and applications* (3rd ed.). Routledge.

Iacobucci, D., Schneider, M. J., Popovich, D. L., & Bakamitsos, G. A. (2016). Mean centering helps alleviate "micro" but not "macro" multicollinearity. *Behavior Research Methods, 48*(4), 1308–1317. https://doi.org/10.3758/s13428-015-0624-x

Jencks, C., & Mayer, S. E. (1990). The social consequences of growing up in a poor neighborhood. In L. E. Lynn & M. G. H. McGeary (Eds.), *Inner-city poverty in the United States* (pp. 111–186). National Academies Press.

Johnson, L. T., Taylor, R. B., & Groff, E. R. (2015, May-June). Metropolitan local crime clusters: Structural concentration effects and the systemic model. *Journal of Criminal Justice, 43*(3), 186–194.

Johnson, N. (2009). *Boardwalk empire: The birth, high times, and corruption of Atlantic City*. Plexus Publishing.

Kaiser, K., & Reisig, M. D. (2017). Legal socialization and self-reported criminal offending: The role of procedural justice and legal orientations. *Journal of Quantitative Criminology*. https://doi.org/10.1007/s10940-017-9375-4

Kelley, J., Evans, M. D. R., Lowman, J., & Lykes, V. (2017). Group-mean-centering independent variables in multi-level models is dangerous. *Quality & Quantity, 51*(1), 261–283. https://doi.org/10.1007/s11135-015-0304-z

Keselman, H. J., & Rogan, J. C. (1978). A comparison of the modified-Tukey and Scheffe methods of multiple comparisons for pairwise contrasts. *Journal of the American Statistical Association, 73*(361), 47–52. https://doi.org/10.2307/2286514

Kohler, U., & Kreuter, F. (2012). *Data analysis using Stata* (3rd ed.). Stata Press.

Kondo, K. (2016). Hot and cold spot analysis using Stata. *Stata Journal, 16*(3), 613–631.

Kreft, I. G., Leeuw, J. D., & Aiken, L. S. (1995). The effect of different forms of centering in hierarchical linear models. *Multivariate Behavioral Research, 30*, 1–21.

Kruschke, J. K. (2011). *Doing Bayesian data analysis*. Elsevier.

Lachenbruch, P. A., & Clements, P. J. (1991). Anova, Kruskal-Wallis, normal scores and unequal variance. *Communications in Statistics – Theory and Methods, 20*(1), 107–126. https://doi.org/10.1080/03610929108830486

Lancaster, T. (2001). The incidental parameter problem since 1948. *Journal of Econometrics, 95*, 391–413.

Lee, V. E. (2000). Using hierarchical linear modeling to study social contexts: The case of school effects. *Educational Psychologist, 35*(2), 125–141. https://doi.org/10.1207/S15326985EP3502_6

Liska, A. E. (1990). The significance of aggregate dependent variables and contextual independent variables for linking macro and micro theories. *Social Psychology Quarterly, 53*(4), 292–301.

Lockwood, B. (2012). The influence of travel distance on treatment noncompletion for juvenile offenders. *Journal of Research in Crime and Delinquency, 49*(4), 572–600. https://doi.org/10.1177/0022427811414198

Lockwood, B., Wyant, B. R., & Grunwald, H. E. (2021). Locating litter: An exploratory multilevel analysis of the spatial patterns of litter in Philadelphia. *Environment and Behavior*, *53*(6), 601–635. https://doi.org/10.1177/0013916520906834

Long, J. S. (1997). *Regression models for categorical and limited dependent variables*. Sage.

Long, J. S. (2009). *The workflow of data analysis using Stata*. Stata Press.

Longest, K. C. (2014). *Using Stata for quantitative analysis* (2nd ed.). Sage.

Luke, D. A. (2004). *Multilevel modeling*. Sage.

MacKinnon, D. P., & Pirlott, A. G. (2015). Statistical approaches for enhancing causal interpretation of the M to Y relation in mediation analysis. *Personality and Social Psychology Review*, *19*(1), 30–43. https://doi.org/10.1177/1088868314542878

Mainland, D. (1954, September). The rise of experimental statistics and the problem of a medical statistician. *Yale Journal of Biology and Medicine*, *27*(1), 1–10.

Malich, L., & Munafò, M. R. (2022). Introduction: Replication of crises – interdisciplinary reflections on the phenomenon of the replication crisis in psychology. *Review of General Psychology*, *26*(2), 127–130. https://doi.org/10.1177/10892680221077997

Masyn, K. E. (2013). Latent class analysis and finite mixture modeling. In T. Little (Ed.), *The Oxford handbook of quantitative methods: Vol. 2. Statistical analysis* (pp. 551–611). Oxford University Press.

McKenzie, R. D. (1923). *The neighborhood: A study of local life in the city of Columbus, Ohio*. University of Chicago Press.

Miethe, T. D., & Meier, R. F. (1994). *Crime and its social context*. SUNY Press.

Nagin, D. (2005). *Group-based modeling of development*. Harvard University Press.

Olvera Astivia, O. L., & Kroc, E. (2019). Centering in multiple regression does not always reduce multicollinearity: How to tell when your estimates will not benefit from centering. *Educational and Psychological Measurement*, *79*(5), 813–826. https://doi.org/10.1177/0013164418817801

Paccagnella, O. (2006). Centering or not centering in multilevel models? The role of the group mean and the assessment of group effects. *Evaluation Review*, *30*(1), 66–85. https://doi.org/10.1177/0193841x05275649

Parker, K. F. (2008). *Unequal crime decline*. New York University Press.

Paternoster, R., Brame, R., Bacon, S., & Ditchfield, A. (2004). Justice by geography and race: The administration of the death penalty in Maryland, 1978–1999. *University of Maryland Law Journal*, *1*, 1–98.

Perkins, D., & Taylor, R. B. (1996). Ecological assessments of disorder: Their relationship to fear of crime and theoretical implications. *American Journal of Community Psychology*, *24*, 63–107.

Pettigrew, T. F. (2018). The emergence of contextual social psychology. *Personality and Social Psychology Bulletin*, *44*(7), 963–971. https://doi.org/10.1177/0146167218756033

Plazzi, A., Torous, W., & Valkanov, R. (2010). Expected returns and expected growth in rents of commercial real estate. *The Review of Financial Studies*, *23*(9), 3469–3519. https://doi.org/10.1093/rfs/hhq069

Preacher, K. J., Zyphur, M. J., & Zhang, Z. (2010). A general multilevel SEM framework for assessing multilevel mediation. *Psychological Methods*, *15*(3), 209–233. https://doi.org/10.1037/a0020141

Rabe-Hesketh, S., & Skrondal, A. (2012a). *Multilevel and longitudinal modeling using Stata: Vol. I. Continuous responses* (3rd ed.). Stata Press.

Rabe-Hesketh, S., & Skrondal, A. (2012b). *Multilevel and longitudinal modeling using Stata: Vol. II. Categorical responses, counts and survival* (3rd ed.). Stata Press.

Raftery, A. E. (1995a). Bayesian model selection in social research. *Sociological Methodology, 25*, 111–163.

Raftery, A. E. (1995b). Rejoinder: Model selection is unavoidable in social research. *Sociological Methodology, 25*, 185–195.

Raudenbush, S. W. (2001). Comparing personal trajectories and drawing causal inferences from longitudinal data. *Annual Review of Psychology, 52*, 501.

Raudenbush, S. W. (2005). How do we study "what happens next"? *Annals of the American Academy of Political and Social Science, 602*, 131–144.

Raudenbush, S. W., & Bryk, A. S. (2002). *Hierarchical linear models: Applications and data analysis methods* (2nd ed.). Sage Publications.

Raymond, E., Wang, K., & Immergluck, D. (2016). Race and uneven recovery: Neighborhood home value trajectories in Atlanta before and after the housing crisis. *Housing Studies, 31*(3), 324–339. https://doi.org/10.1080/02673037.2015.1080821

Robson, K., & Pevalin, D. (2016). *Multilevel modeling in plain language.* Sage.

Sampson, R. J. (2012). *Great American city: Chicago and the enduring neighborhood effect.* University of Chicago Press.

Sampson, R. J., Morenoff, J. D., & Gannon-Rowley, T. (2002). Assessing "neighborhood effects": Social processes and new directions in research. *Annual Review of Sociology, 28*, 443–478.

Sampson, R. J., Raudenbush, S. W., & Earls, F. (1997). Neighborhoods and violent crime: A multi-level study of collective efficacy. *Science, 277*, 918–924.

Scheffe, H. (1959). *The analysis of variance.* Wiley & Sons.

Schmidt-Catran, A. W., & Spies, D. C. (2016). Immigration and welfare support in Germany. *American Sociological Review, 81*(2), 242–261. https://doi.org/10.1177/0003122416633140

Sharkey, P., & Faber, J. W. (2014). Where, when, why, and for whom do residential contexts matter? Moving away from the dichotomous understanding of neighborhood effects. *Annual Review of Sociology, 40*, 559–579. https://doi.org/10.1146/annurev-soc-071913-043350

Shieh, Y.-Y., & Fouladi, R. T. (2003). The effect of multicollinearity on multilevel modeling parameter estimates and standard errors. *Educational and Psychological Measurement, 63*(6), 951–985. https://doi.org/10.1177/0013164403258402

Shinn, M. (1990). Mixing and matching: Levels of conceptualization, measurement, and statistical analysis in community research. In P. Tolan, C. Keys, F. Chertok, & L. Jason (Eds.), *Researching community psychology: Issues of theory and methods* (pp. 111–126). American Psychological Association.

Shrout, P. E., & Fleiss, J. L. (1979). Intraclass correlations: Uses in assessing rater reliability. *Psychological Bulletin, 86*(2), 420–428.

Silverstein, S. (2004). *Where the sidewalk ends: The poems and drawings of Shel Silverstein* (30th anniversary special ed.). Harper Collins. (Original work published 1974)

Skardhamar, T. (2010). Distinguishing facts and artifacts in group-based modeling. *Criminology, 48*(1), 295–320.

Skrondal, A., & Rabe-Hesketh, S. (2003). Multilevel logistic regression for polytomous data and rankings. *Psychometrika, 68*(2), 267–287.

Snijders, T. A. B., & Bosker, R. J. (1994). *Multilevel analysis: An introduction to basic and advanced multilevel modeling.* Sage.

Snijders, T. A. B., & Bosker, R. J. (2012). *Multilevel analysis: An introduction to basic and advanced multilevel modeling* (2nd ed.). Sage.

Sorg, E. T., & Taylor, R. B. (2011). Community-level impacts of temperature on urban street robbery. *Journal of Criminal Justice, 39*(6), 463–470. https://doi.org/10.1016/j.jcrimjus.2011.08.004

Spybrook, J., Bloom, H., Congdon, R., Hill, C., Martinez, A., & Raudenbush, S. W. (2011). *Optimal design plus empirical evidence: Documentation for the "optimal design" software version 3.0.* Retrieved March 30, 2019, from http://wtgrantfoundation.org/resource/optimal-design-with-empirical-information-od

Stewart, I. (1996). Monopoly revisited. *Scientific American, 275*(4), 116–119.

Suttles, G. D. (1972). *The social construction of communities.* University of Chicago Press.

Taylor, R. B. (1994). *Research methods in criminal justice.* McGraw Hill.

Taylor, R. B. (2015). *Community criminology: Fundamentals of spatial and temporal scaling, ecological indicators, and selectivity bias.* New York University Press.

Taylor, R. B., Kelly, C., E., & Salvatore, C. (2010). Where concerned citizens perceive police as more responsive to troublesome teen groups: Theoretical implications for political economy, incivilities and policing. *Policing & Society, 20*(2), 143–171.

Tienda, M. (1991). Poor people in poor places: Deciphering neighborhood effects on poverty outcomes. In J. Huber (Ed.), *Macro-micro linkages in sociology* (pp. 244–262). Sage.

Townsley, M. (2009). Spatial autocorrelation and impacts on criminology. *Geographical Analysis, 41*(4), 452–461. https://doi.org/10.1111/j.1538-4632.2009.00775.x

Trafimow, D., & Marks, M. (2015). Editorial. *Basic and Applied Social Psychology, 37*(1), 1–2. https://doi.org/10.1080/01973533.2015.1012991

Troy, A., & Grove, J. M. (2008). Property values, parks, and crime: A hedonic analysis in Baltimore, MD. *Landscape and Urban Planning, 87*(3), 233–245.

Tukey, J. W. (1957). On the comparative anatomy of transformations. *The Annals of Mathematical Statistics, 28*(3), 602–632.

Tukey, J. W. (1977). *Exploratory data analysis.* Addison Wesley.

Twisk, J. W. R. (2013). *Applied longitudinal data analysis for epidemiology* (2nd ed.). Cambridge University Press.

Ulmer, J. T., & Bradley, M. S. (2006). Variation in trial penalties among serious violent offenses. *Criminology, 44*, 631–670.

Van den Noortgate, W., López-López, J. A., Marín-Martínez, F., & Sánchez-Meca, J. (2015). Meta-analysis of multiple outcomes: A multilevel approach. *Behavior Research Methods, 47*(4), 1274–1294. https://doi.org/10.3758/s13428-014-0527-2

Vrieze, S. I. (2012). Model selection and psychological theory: A discussion of the differences between the Akaike information criterion (AIC) and the Bayesian information criterion (BIC). *Psychological Methods, 17*(2), 228–243.

Warner, S. B. (1962). *Streetcar suburbs: The process of growth in Boston, 1870–1900.* Harvard University Press.

Weisburd, D., Bushway, S., Lum, C., & Yang, S. M. (2004). Trajectories of crime at places: A longitudinal study of street segments in the city of Seattle. *Criminology, 42*(2), 283–321.

Weisburd, D., Groff, E. R., & Yang, S.-M. (2012). *The criminology of place: Street segments and our understanding of the crime problem.* Oxford University Press.

Weisz, J. R., Kuppens, S., Eckshtain, D., Ugueto, A. M., Hawley, K. M., & Jensen-Doss, A. (2013). Performance of evidence-based youth psychotherapies compared with usual clinical care: A multilevel meta-analysis. *JAMA Psychiatry, 70*(7), 750–761. https://doi.org/10.1001/jamapsychiatry.2013.1176

Welch, T. F., Gehrke, S. R., & Farber, S. (2018). Rail station access and housing market resilience: Case studies of Atlanta, Baltimore and Portland. *Urban Studies, 55*(16), 3615–3630.

White, H. (1982). Maximum likelihood estimation of mis-specified models. *Econometrica, 50*(1–25).

Wilcox, P., Land, K. C., & Hunt, S. A. (2003). *Criminal circumstance: A dynamic multicontextual criminal opportunity theory.* Aldine deGruyter.

Winfield, A. M. (1919). *The Rover Boys under canvas or the mystery of the wrecked submarine.* Grosset & Dunlap.

Wooldridge, J. M. (2002). *Econometric analysis of cross section and panel data.* MIT Press.

Wyant, B. R. (2008). Multilevel impacts of perceived incivilities and perceptions of crime risk on fear of crime. *Journal of Research in Crime and Delinquency, 45*(1), 39–64.

Yang, Y. (2005). Can the strengths of AIC and BIC be shared? A conflict between model identification and regression estimation. *Biometrika, 92*(4), 937–950.

Zangger, C. (2019). Making a place for space: Using spatial econometrics to model neighborhood effects. *Journal of Urban Affairs, 41*(8), 1055–1080. https://doi.org/10.1080/07352166.2019.1584530

Index

For Product Safety Concerns and Information please contact our EU
representative GPSR@taylorandfrancis.com
Taylor & Francis Verlag GmbH, Kaufingerstraße 24, 80331 München, Germany

www.ingramcontent.com/pod-product-compliance
Lightning Source LLC
Chambersburg PA
CBHW050715280326
41926CB00088B/3035

9 781032 492186